Learning 06

怎樣寫好英文作文

基 礎 入 門 篇

吳奕真／主編

張先信 · **Phillip Podgur**／編著

序

　　英語教學要培養四種基本能力：聽的能力、閱讀能力、口頭表達能力和文字表達能力。正常的英語教學，應該發揮這四種功能。在考試領導教學的情形下，對於中學生英文寫作能力的培養，荒廢已久，現在大專聯考加考英文作文，將有助於英文教學的正常化，充分實現這門課程的多元目標。在這一方面，我想最重要的是按照正常程序教學，不必有什麼大更張，很自然而輕鬆地培養起學生的英文文字表達能力，不要剛從一種偏差回過頭來，又鑽進一個新的牛角尖。

　　一項學習活動，要由希望獲得的成果來決定。英文的口頭表達能力和筆寫表達能力，各有其不同的培養途徑。就筆寫表達能力而言，最根本的辦法當然是從培養語言習慣做起，很自然地養成基本的表達能力。但是在目前我國英語教學的客觀條件之下，似乎還不容易很圓滿地做到這一點。而且口說的語言和筆寫的文字之間總是有些距離的。一種外國語的學習，本來就是一個記憶和模仿的過程，不論是有意的，還是無意的。口語如此，文字的表達亦然。在文字的表達方面，需要更為嚴密的組織和正確無訛的形式，就是要字斟句酌；這種能力的培養，就我國中學生而言，更有賴於有意的記憶和模仿。

　　要想寫出清通的合乎習慣用法的英文，至少要熟讀若干篇適當的文章，融會貫通，熟諳基本的句法和常用的成語，到作文的時候才能做靈活的運用，正確而有效地表達出自己的意思。把這個基礎打好，可以終身受用。事實上，中學的英文課本裡面的文章應該是很好的模仿

對象，不過有些教材可能與現實生活環境有些距離，或文體比較老式，因而效果不彰。老一輩的人從前在小學和初中時代要學作文言文。怎樣才能作文言文呢？不二的法門就是先熟讀若干篇文章，如《飲冰室文集》之類作品，爛熟胸中，自然就能下筆自如。現在中學生作英文作文，頗有類於從前小學生學作文言文。要熟讀範文，才會作文。當然每次背誦的份量不能太多，以免構成學生的過重負荷，產生不良作用。

　　本書的編著，就是希望能就英文作文提供一種比較實用的教材或讀物，以求達成學習的效果。全書分為基礎入門篇和應用進階篇，基礎入門篇討論句子和段落，所提供的例文和例句，都儘量選取文字簡練、難易適度、內容豐富有意義的文字，其中很多可以當作模仿的對象。並附有豐富的練習，使學生得以培養基本的寫作能力。在最後的「總練習」裡，我們提供二十個作文題目，每個題目下面並附有提示，供學生練習寫作八十字左右的短文。應用進階篇討論全篇的英文作文，提供範文二十三篇，有些篇是由編著者撰寫的，有些篇是改寫的，屬於四種不同的體裁，內容採用中國本位，儘量以中學生的現實生活為題材。對字彙和成語加以控制，並使之重複出現，每篇均詳加注釋，對成語用法提供例句。為便利教學並供學生自修起見，範文均附有中文翻譯。每篇後面的練習分為三部分：第一部分是問答，幫助學生嫻熟範文內容。第二部分是中譯英，由學生練習使用本課學過的成語。第三部分是作文。作文的長度請教師斟酌決定，大致可分為三個階段：第一階段每篇以二百字為度，第二階段三百字，第三階段四百字或更多。

　　本書對於作文方法只做概要的敘述，並就每篇範文的結構略作評釋。在這一方面，學生只要能達到最基本的要求就好了。中學生在中文作文方面已有相當的經驗；就文章做法而言，中文和英文是一樣的。在目前這個階段，最重要的是訓練學生寫出通順英文的能力，進一步的寫作技巧，不妨留待大學裡面的英文作文課程來培養。

　　張先信教授在國立臺灣師範大學英語系講授英文作文多年，在這方面具有豐富的經驗。師大英語系美籍講師白非力先生（Phillip Podgur）　本書備有習題解答，專供參考之用。

　　本書於編著及校訂過程中雖極審慎，疏漏之處仍屬難免，尚希方家惠予指正。

吳奚真

目　　錄

第一章　句子的形式

第一節　甚麼叫做句子

　　句子（sentence）是構成一篇作文的基本單位。英文的句子是按照文法（grammar）和造句法（syntax）的規則而形成的一組字，用以表達一個完整或近乎完整的意思。一般說來，句子的第一個字母應該大寫；句子的末尾應該有個句號 (.)、問號 (?) 或感嘆號 (!)。除了命令句、祈使句、感嘆句或非正式的用法以外，一個完整的句子應該有主詞（subject）和述詞（predicate）。句子的主詞可能是名詞（noun）、代名詞（pronoun）或名詞相等詞（noun equivalents）。句子的述詞除了動詞以外，可能還有受詞（object）或補語（complement）。動詞可能是一般動詞（verb），也可能是連繫動詞（linking verb）。受詞又分為直接受詞（direct object）和間接受詞（indirect object）。補語可能是主詞補語（subject complement），也可能是受詞補語（object complement）。

　　請仔細閱讀下面這篇談集郵的短文：

STAMP　COLLECTING

Stamp collecting is a very interesting and useful hobby. You can learn many things about geography and history from stamps. Today more people collect stamps than ever before, and special stamps are often printed for these people. If you buy a new stamp and put it on an envelope on the first day it is sold, the envelope may be worth a lot of money in the future. Many stamp collectors go to the post office when new stamps are being sold. They put the new stamp on an envelope and then mail the envelope to themselves.

People all over the world like collecting stamps. Indeed, some doctors say that everybody is fond of collecting something. Some children enjoy collecting matchboxes and others like collecting coins. Collecting paintings is a hobby of many rich men, but they often do this to make money. They keep the painting for a period of time and then sell it at a much higher price. Collecting paintings is business to them. Collecting stamps, also, can be a kind of business. You may be lucky in finding a 'special' stamp on an old letter. This 'special' stamp may be worth a lot of money.

上面這篇短文一共有十五個句子，每個句子都以大寫字母開始，如第一段第一句的 Stamp collecting；每個句子的末尾都有一個句號

(.)；每個句子都有主詞，如第一段第二句的You；每個句子都有述詞，如第二段第一句的like collecting stamps。今將上文中的簡單句（simple sentence）按主詞和述詞兩部分排列如下，以表明句子的基本形式。

主　詞	述　詞
Stamp collecting	is a very interesting and useful hobby.
You	can learn many things about geography and history from stamps.
They	put the new stamp on an envelope and then mail the envelope to themselves.
People all over the world	like collecting stamps.
They	keep the painting for a period of time and then sell it at a much higher price.
Collecting paintings	is business to them.
Collecting stamps,	also, can be a kind of business.
You	may be lucky in finding a 'special' stamp on an old letter.
This 'special' stamp	may be worth a lot of money.

練 習 一

將下列各句分成主詞和述詞兩部分。

例：

主　詞	述　詞
One of my classmates	is from southern Taiwan.
	has lived in Taipei for two years.

1. The boy worked very hard.

2. She helped her mother after school.

3. His father ran a small barbershop.

4. A box of pencils is lying on the desk.

5. A salesman knocked at the door one afternoon.

6. She is an unusually talented pianist.

7. A boy with a fine mind should continue his education.

8. The two women looked at each other sadly.

9. He should take a full-time job now.

10. The little girl in the cottage looked out from the window.

11. His friends came to his aid.

12. They raised ten thousand dollars for him.

13. The old woman lay in bed quietly.

14. Most of the leaves have fallen.

15. They were married before long.

16. Their friendship was based on mutual honesty and trust.

17. The energetic young man achieved one success after another.

18. People breathlessly waited for the outcome of the race.

19. Cheering crowds of people lined the streets.

20. He was, indeed, a very famous man.

第二節　敍述句、疑問句、祈使句、感嘆句

按照句子的含義和詞序（word order），我們可以把句子分為敍述句（declarative sentence）、疑問句（interrogative sentence）、祈使句（imperative sentence）和感嘆句（exclamatory sentence）。

Ⅰ.敍述句

敍述句主要是用來敍述一個事實，有時也可以用來敍述一件可能的事或一件不可能的事。我們平常所用的句子大部分都是敍述句。敍述句的末尾要用句號。例如：

Abraham Lincoln was a great man.

We are all in the same boat now.

They will probably leave on Sunday.

It is impossible for man to live without air.

在這四個句子當中，第一、二句敍述一個事實，第三句敍述一件可能的事，第四句敍述一件不可能的事。

敍述句的詞序是〔主詞+動詞〕（subject + verb），也就是說，敍述句的主詞通常出現在句子的開頭。不過，有時候敍述句的開頭可能是個副詞片語，主詞反而出現在句子的末尾，如 Beyond the Alps lies Italy。

Ⅱ.疑問句

所謂疑問句，通常是指用來發問的句子。疑問句可分為〔是或不〕

問句（yes-no question）、疑問詞問句（wh-question）、選擇性問句（choice question）和附加問句（tag question）。疑問句的末尾要用問號。例如：

1. Is Bob studying?

2. Does Jim want to go?

3. Has Jane made a mistake?

4. Who put it there?

5. What did you do after that?

6. When did you see it last?

7. Where are you from?

8. Why are you going to town?

9. Do you want this book or that one?

10. Would you like coffee, tea, or milk?

11. Mary is a good girl, isn't she?

12. This book isn't very difficult, is it?

〔是或不〕問句是由連繫動詞（linking verb）或助動詞（auxiliary verb）開始的，如第一至第三句。此種問句以 yes 或 no 開始作答，如果答案是肯定的，就以 yes 開始作答；如果答案是否定的，就以 no 開始作答。

疑問詞問句是由疑問詞 who, whose, whom, what, when ,why, where, which, how 等開始的，如第四至八句。由於這種問句是用來打聽消息的，所以又叫做消息問句（information question）。疑問詞問句不能以 yes 或 no 開始作答，必須直接用敘述句來回答。

　　選擇性問句是用來提出兩個或更多的事物供對方選擇的,如第九至十句,此種問句的詞序與〔是或不〕問句相似,但不能用 yes 或 no 開始作答,而必須就問句中所提出的事物擇一回答,或另作適當的回答。

　　附加問句是接在敘述句後面的簡短問句,如第十一至十二句。此種問句主要是用來徵求對方的同意的。在這種問句中,敘述句若是肯定的,附加問句必是否定的;敘述句若是否定的,附加問句必是肯定的。

Ⅲ. 祈使句

　　祈使句是用來表示命令或請求的。這種句子末尾通常用句號,有時也可用感嘆號。例如:

1. Get out of here.

2. Stay in bed.

3. Be ready at dawn.

4. Write more distinctly!

5. Run quickly!

6. Have another cup of tea.

7. Shut the door, please.

8. Turn left, please.

　　以上的八個句子都是典型的祈使句,第一至五句表示命令,第六至八句表示請求。在典型的祈使句中,動詞用原形,沒有數和時態的變化,主詞 you 常被省略。

IV. 感嘆句

感嘆句是用來表示強烈感情的。此種句子常以 what 和 how 開始，修飾句中的補語或受詞。感嘆句的末尾用驚嘆號。例如：

What a wonderful singer Tom is!

What a mistake he made!

What a time we had today!

What a mess we're in!

How delightful her manners are!

How cold it is!

以 what 和 how 開始的感嘆句常常略去動詞，有時主詞亦可省略，僅僅保留表示感嘆的部分。例如：

What a terrible mistake!

How encouraging!

練 習 二

A. 仔細閱讀下面這篇文章：

SWIMMING IS FOR YOUNG AND OLD

Men have been swimming for a long time. Thousands of years ago men swam to get away from enemies and wild animals. They swam in ponds, lakes, rivers, and oceans. Now people swim for fun

and exercise. Most cities have public pools and swimming lessons for people of all ages.

Some people are afraid of learning to swim. Non-swimmers think that their bodies will not float. This is not true. Bodies float naturally. Most people can learn to swim if they try.

Babies less than one year old have learned to swim. They are called 'water babies'. Some babies have learned to swim even before they learned to walk.

People who study about body health believe that swimming can slow down signs of aging. Swimming is especially good for the heart and lungs. When a person swims he breathes more deeply. His heart also beats faster. Then blood can be sent more easily to all parts of the body. Swimming has helped many people look young and healthy.

When swimming and diving, people should be careful. Swimming in a place that has no lifeguard can be dangerous. Always go swimming with a friend.

B. 將下列各敘述句改寫成〔是或不〕問句：

例：This exercise is helpful. →

Is this exercise helpful? →

Mr. Lin can speak English well.

Can Mr. Lin speak English well?

1. Men have been swimming for a long time.

2. People swim for fun and exercise.

3. Most cities have public pools.

4. Some people are afraid of learning to swim.

5. It is true that bodies float naturally.

6. Most people can learn to swim if they try.

7. Babies less than one year old can learn to swim.

8. Some babies can learn to swim before they learn to walk.

9. Swimming can slow down signs of aging.

10. Swimming is good for the heart and lungs.

11. Swimming has helped many people look young and healthy.

12. People should be careful when swimming and diving.

13. Swimming in a place that has no lifeguard is dangerous.

14. You should always go swimming with a friend.

C. 用下列各單字或片語各造一個敘述句（所造的句子不能與A部分選文中的句子完全相同）：

怎樣寫好 英文 作文

1. swim　v.　游泳

2. get away from　逃避

3. (do something) for fun　當作消遣

4. exercise　n.　運動

5. public　adj.　公共的；公用的

6. afraid of　害怕

7. float　v.　漂浮

8. try　v.　嘗試

9. learn　v.　學習

10. study　v.　研究

11. believe　v.　相信；認為

12. slow down　減退；減慢

13. help　v.　促使；幫助

14. send　v.　送達

15. careful　adj.　小心；當心

16. dangerous　adj.　危險的

練 習 三

A. 仔細閱讀下面這篇文章：

THE FATHER AND
HIS SONS

A father had three sons, but the boys were always quarreling among themselves. The father wanted all his sons to be kind to one another, and he called them to him.

He showed them three sticks and said, "I want to talk to you. Take these sticks and tie them together. Then try to break the bundle of sticks."

The oldest son tried with all his strength, but he could not break it. Then the other two tried, but neither of them could break it.

"Now," said the father, "untie the bundle and each of you take one stick and try to break it."

Each of them could break the stick easily. Then the father said, "My sons, when the sticks are tied together, the bundle is very strong, and you cannot break it. But when they are not tied together, you

can break each stick easily. When you work together and help one another, you can become as strong as the bundle. But if you only quarrel and do not help one another, you will be broken as easily as each of these sticks."

B.　根據上面的文章，用完整的句子回答下列各問題：

1.　How many sons did the father have?

2.　Were they always quarreling?

3.　What did their father try to do?

4.　What did their father show them?

5.　What did the father ask his sons to do with the sticks?

6.　How hard did the oldest son try?

7.　Could the oldest son break the bundle of sticks?

8.　Could the other two break it?

9.　What did the father ask his sons to do next?

10.　Could each son break the stick easily?

11.　According to their father, how could the brothers become as strong as the bundle?

12.　What would happen if the brothers only quarreled and did not help one another?

C. 用下列各單字或片語各造一個敘述句、疑問句、祈使句或感嘆句：

1. quarrel   v.   爭吵

2. call   v.   召喚

3. show   v.   拿給……看

4. want   v.   想要

5. talk   v.   談話

6. take   v.   拿走；帶走

7. tie   v.   捆綁

8. break   v.   折斷

9. strength   n.   力氣；力量

10. untie   v.   解開

11. strong   adj.   堅固的；結實的

12. work   v.   工作

13. become   v.   變得

14. one another   互相

15. bundle   n.   捆

第三節　簡單句、集合句、複合句、混合句

按照句子所含子句的數目和種類，我們可以把句子分為簡單句（simple sentence）、集合句（compound sentence）、複合句（complex sentence）及混合句（compound-complex sentence）。

Ⅰ.簡單句

所謂簡單句，就是指僅僅含有一個主要子句（main clause）而沒有附屬子句（subordinate clause）的句子；簡單句通常只有一個主詞和一個述詞。請仔細閱讀下面這篇文章：

BELLOW THE WRITER

Saul Bellow is one of America's best living writers. Some people say he is one of the world's best living writers. Bellow was born sixty-five years ago in Canada. His parents were Russian Jews. When Bellow was a boy his family moved to Chicago. Because he grew up there, Bellow feels that Chicago is his true home. As he grew up, Bellow learned several foreign languages. He graduated from college in 1937. After graduation, he soon decided that he wanted to be a writer.

In his novels, Bellow often writes about

experiences from his own life. He is very familiar with life on the streets of Chicago. Chicago is the setting for several of his novels. Bellow's Jewish background is also an important influence on his writing. His writing style is sometimes funny, sometimes serious. It is always entertaining.

The characters in Bellow's novels generally have the feeling that they are outside of society. Their struggles to make sense of the world and themselves form the basis of Bellow's novels. His characters are not always completely successful, but because of this they are very human.

上面這篇文章中共有十一個簡單句：

1. Saul Bellow is one of America's best living writers.

2. Bellow was born sixty-five years ago in Canada.

3. His parents were Russian Jews.

4. Bellow graduated from college in 1937.

5. In his novels, Bellow often writes about experiences from his own life.

6. He is very familiar with life on the streets of Chicago.

7. Chicago is the setting for several of his novels.

8. Bellow's Jewish background is also an important influence on his writing.

9. His writing style is sometimes funny, sometimes serious.

10. It is always entertaining.

11. Their struggles to make sense of the world and themselves form the basis of Bellow's novels.

不過，簡單句可以有複合主詞（compound subject）。

例如：

John and *Tom* are bitter enemies.

Men, *women* and *children* shouted and screamed.

簡單句也可以有複合述詞（compound predicate）。

例如：

The guests *talked* and *laughed*.

The airplane *landed*, *refueled*, and *took off* again.

簡單句也可以包含分詞片語（participial phrase）。

例如：

Smiling happily, she began to sing.

The ships, *being built of steel*, are light and strong.

簡單句不一定都很短。它可以短得只有兩個字；也可以很長。

例如：

Birds fly.

Birds from all parts of the South fly to distant valleys and mountains of the North in the months of March, April and May.

練 習 四

A. 仔細閱讀下面這篇文章，選出其中的簡單句，並按順序寫下來：

LIVING IN BEAUTY

Bernard Berenson was only a child when his grandmother died. Yet her death had a profound effect on him. To him, death was the worst of all evils. He thought that it would be better to be a stick or a stone because sticks and stones don't die. But on the other hand, sticks and stones don't live either. Anything, he concluded, would be better than not to have lived.

And live he did! His life became somewhat of a legend. He was born in Europe in 1865. His early years in Europe instilled in him a deep joy for life. This joy, however, was often tested during his first years in the United States.

Berenson's family immigrated to the United States in 1875. His father became a wandering peddler in Boston. Young Berenson spent most of his time studying in a city he found ugly and

painful.

The studying paid off. He won a scholarship to Harvard and upon graduating in 1887, he was sent to Europe to study art history.

Through writing books, selling, buying and telling others about the great masterpieces of Italian art, Berenson brought joy and beauty to other people.

B. 用下列單字及片語各造一個簡單句：

1. die   v.   死

2. profound   adj.   深厚的；深刻的

3. become   v.   變成

4. evil   n.   罪惡

5. spend   v.   花費

6. belong to   屬於

7. joy   n.   快樂，欣喜

8. test   v.   試驗；考驗

9. immigrate   v.   移居

10. pay off   有報償；沒有白費

Ⅱ. 集合句

　　集合句是由兩個或更多的主要子句組成的，請仔細閱讀下面這篇文章：

THIS I BELIEVE

　　All men cannot be masters, but none need be a slave. We cannot cast out pain from the world, but needless suffering we can. Tragedy will be with us in some degree as long as there is life, but misery we can banish. Injustice will raise its head in the possible worlds, but tyranny we can conquer. Evil will invade some men's hearts, intolerence will twist some men's minds, but decency is a far more common human attribute and it can be made to prevail in our daily lives.

　　I have known, as who has not, personal disappointments and despair. But always the thought of tomorrow has buoyed me up. I have looked to the future all life. I still do. I still believe with courage and intelligence we can make the future bright with fulfilment.

上面這篇文章有四個集合句：

1. All men cannot be masters, *but* none need be a slave.

2. We cannot cast out pain from the world, *but* needless suffering we can.

3. Injustice will raise its head in the possible worlds, *but* tyranny we can conquer.

4. Evil will invade some men's hearts, intolerence will twist some men's minds, *but* decency is a far more common human attribute *and* it can be made to prevail in our daily lives.

　　上面這四個集合句中的主要子句都是用對等連接詞and和but連接起來的。集合句中的主要子句也可用其他的對等連接詞for, or, so, nor, yet等來連接，如下面的第一至五句。集合句中的子句有時也可用分號（semicolon）加連接副詞（conjunctive adverb）來連接，如下面的第六句。有時也用對等連接詞加連接副詞來連接，如下面的第七句。有時根本不用連接詞而只用分號來連接，如下面的第八句。假如集合句中的子句很短而且關係很密切時，則只用逗號（comma）來連接就夠了，如下面的第九句。

1. It will rain, *for* the barometer is falling.

2. Sue can't be very ill *or* she wouldn't have come.

3. He can't do it, *nor* can I.

4. He had a headache, *so* he went to bed.

5. Jim tried hard, *yet* he didn't succeed.

6. We kept ringing the bell for several minutes; *however*, there was no answer.

7. The meeting ended at seven in the evening, *and consequently* we had to hurry to catch our train.

8. I turned on the cold water; it was most refreshing.

9. Some students carry lunch to school, others eat in a cafeteria.

注意：for 和 because 的用法不同。because 是附屬連接詞，引導出一個附屬子句，表明實際的原因；for是對等連接詞，引導出一個主要（或獨立）子句，這個主要子句並不表明實際的原因，而只是提供一個邏輯上的理由，作為一種佐證，證明前一個子句裡所述是真實的。例如：

The Browns became people of wealth *because* they saved their money and invested it wisely. (Dependent clause of cause)

The Browns must be people of wealth, *for* they go abroad every year. (Independent clause of reason)

for 不用於句首，前面要用逗號；because 有時可用於句首，不用於句首時，前面可以不用逗號，也可以用逗號。例如：

Because he is ill, he is absent today.

He is absent today *because* he is ill.

He must be ill , *for* he is absent today.

練 習 五

A. 仔細閱讀下面這篇文章，找出其中的集合句，並按照順序寫下來：

DR. SUN YAT-SEN, FOUNDER OF THE REPUBLIC OF CHINA

In 1896 Dr. Sun Yat-sen visited England. One Sunday morning he was walking down a street in London on his way to church when two Chinese men suddenly came up to him.

"Excuse me, sir, are you Japanese?" one of the men asked.

"No, I'm Chinese, I come from Canton," Dr. Sun laughed.

"We come from canton ourselves," the other man said. "Come to our house for a few minutes. It's just around the corner."

"But I'm on my way to church," Dr. Sun replied.

"We only want to have a short talk with you. It won't take long," the man said.

Dr. Sun agreed and went inside a large house nearby. When he was in the house, the two men attacked him and pushed him into a small room at the top of the house. There were iron bars over the small window of the room. Dr. Sun was a prisoner! The two men had played a trick on him. Every day Dr. Sun threw notes out of the window down to the street below. In the notes he asked his friends to help him, but it was useless. Then at last an English servant in the house agreed to take a note to his friends. Soon many important people all over the world learned that Dr. Sun was a prisoner in London. In a week he was set free.

During the nest sixteen years Dr. Sun visited many countries, and he gathered together the Chinese people who lived in those countries. He talked to people about the great need for a new government in China and he collected money to fight the old government. Sometimes he disguised himself and paid secret visits to China. He never stopped working and making plans for a better China. In the year 1911 the old government of China was overthrown and a democratic one was

established. Dr. Sun became the first president of China, but there was still much quarreling. Even when Dr. Sun died in 1925, he thought that he had failed. But he was wrong. Although he did not know it, he had helped to build a new China.

B.　按照下列各中文句子的意思各造一個集合句：

1.　昨天很熱，所以我們去游泳。

2.　我很喜歡游泳，而且我游得很好。

3.　學游泳並不難，但需要經常練習。

4.　我妹妹很想買那個玩具，但她沒有足夠的錢。

5.　我昨天晚上睡得很遲，所以今天早上十點才起來。

6.　他不覺得恐懼，因為他是一個勇敢的人。

Ⅲ. 複合句

　　所謂複合句，就是指含有一個主要子句，一個或更多附屬子句的句子。附屬子句又分為名詞子句（noun clause），形容詞子句（adjective clause）和副詞子句（adverbial clause）。請仔細閱讀下面這段文字：

There was a game of Blind-man's buff. And I cannot believe that David really could not see. You should have seen the way he went after his fat sister in the silk dress! He knocked over the table, fell over

the chairs and hit the piano. Wherever she went, he went too. He always knew where his sister was! He would not catch anyone else. Some of the other players fell against him, but he did not catch them! He went away at once following his fat sister. She often cried out that is was not fair, and it really was not, And when at last he caught her, he pretended he did not know who she was!

上面這段文字有五個句子是複合句：

1. And I cannot believe that David really could not see.
2. You should have seen the way he went after his fat sister in the silk dress!
3. Wherever she went, he went too.
4. He always knew where his sister was!
5. And when at last he caught her, he pretended he did not know who she was!

在第一句中，And I cannot believe 為主要子句，that David really could not see 為名詞子句，做 believe 的受詞。在第二句中，You should have seen the way 為主要子句，he went after his fat sister in the silk dress為形容詞子句，形容the way。在第三句中，he went too 為主要子句，Wherever she went為副詞子句，修飾主要子句的動詞went。第四句中，He always knew為主要子句，where his sister was為名詞子

句,做knew的受詞。第五句雖然不算長,卻含有一個主要子句he pretended,一個副詞子句 when at last he caught her,兩個名詞子句 he did not know 及 who she was;前面一個名詞子句 he did not know 為 pretended 的受詞,後面一個名詞子句 who she was 則為 know 的受詞。

　　複合句中的關係詞(relatives)或附屬連接詞 that 有時可以省略。例如:

You should have seen the way (in which) he went after his fat sister in the silk dress!

And when at last he caught her, he pretended (that) he did not know who she was!

　　就中國學生來說,最應該注意的是複合句,要對這類句子多下工夫,務求精通熟練。

練 習 六

A.　仔細閱讀下面這篇文章,選出其中的複合句,按照順序寫下來,並說明其中每個附屬子句的用法:

A FORGOTTEN ART

Nowadays most people go to markets or modern supermarkets when they want to buy food.

Modern man has forgotten how to survive in the wilderness where there are no markets.

The wilderness is full of plants and animals which can be eaten. But before someone eats these wild foods, he must first learn to follow one very important rule of the wilderness. This rule is that you must never eat a plant until you are certain that it is not harmful.

There are very few places which do not yield some edible plant at least once a year. Many of the cacti which grow in the deserts can be eaten if they are properly prepared. First the thorns must be removed. This can be done either by peeling them away or burning them off. The cactus can then be cut into strips and fried for a tasty meal. Sometimes the heart and the seeds of a cactus can be eaten, too.

Plants are only one side of what the wilderness has to offer. Many animals, like porcupines and squirrels, can provide meat for a wilderness dinner.

The wilderness has a lot to offer to modern man. If we follow the rules, we can once more discover the richness of nature's table.

B. 按照下列各中文句子的意思各造一個複合句:

1. 有很多人仍舊到食品雜貨店去買食品。

2. 你何不到那家超級市場去,那兒正在大減價?

3. 這個湖裡有很多可以吃的魚。

4. 這是他特地為你買的禮物。

5. 他十分感謝你為他所做的一切。

6. 他一到家就會給你電話的。

IV. 混合句

所謂混合句,就是含有兩個或更多的主要子句以及一個或更多的附屬子句的句子。例如:

1. When we listen, we hear; when we look, we see.

2. Our friends, who had gone earlier, promised that they would meet us; but when we arrived at the theater, they were nowhere to be seen.

上面第一句包含兩個主要子句、兩個附屬子句;兩個主要子句為 we hear 及 we see;兩個附屬子句為 when we listen 及 when we look;本句的兩個對等部分係用分號隔開的。第二句包含兩個主要子句、三個附屬子句;兩個主要子句為 Our friends… promised 及 but… they were nowhere to be seen;三個附屬子句為 who had gone earlier, that they would meet us 及 when we arrived at the theater; who had gone earlier 為非限制性形容詞子句,形容 Our friends; that they would meet us 為名詞子句,作 promised 的受詞;when we arrived at the theater 為副詞子句,修飾後

面的主要子句 they were nowhere to be seen;本句的兩個對等部分也是用分號隔開的。

練 習 七

A. 仔細閱讀下面這篇文章，選出其中的混合句，並按照順序寫下來：

THE ROOTS OF PAIN

A human's ability to feel pain helps insure his survival. Pain causes people to withdraw from, or avoid, harmful situations and environments. Pain also forces people to get the rest they need for healing. It is very difficult to conduct research on pain because researchers must rely on the subjective impressions of pain sufferers. After all, pain is the *psychological* experience that one associates with injury or some other type of damage to the body. Individuals subjected to the same stimulus will often experience different levels of pain. The exact reasons for this remain unclear, but it is known that age, sex, and occupation affect one's sensitivity to pain. In general, women are more sensitive to pain

than men; office workers are more sensitive than manual workers.

Physical factors are not always responsible for inducing pain. Emotional disorders can either be the source of discomfort, or they may increase existing physical pain. The persistent muscle tension that accompanies anxiety is thought to be a wide-spread source of pain and a vicious circle can develop: anxiety produces tension, tension produces pain, pain results in alarm and more anxiety, more anxiety results in more pain, and so on....

The relief of pain is not always a simple matter. In cases of severe pain due to physical problems, doctors rely on special drugs or surgery. Pain caused by an emotional problem is handled by eliminating the source of anxiety. Once anxiety is eliminated, the accompanying pain usually ceases.

B. 按照下列各中文句子的意思各造一個混合句：

1. 她生日那天她父親送給她一隻手錶，她母親送給他一個洋娃娃，那個洋娃娃看起來跟真人一樣。

2. 他有兩個哥哥；她大哥是醫生，目前在臺北市一家醫院工作，他二哥是律師，目前在高雄市開業。

第二章　基本句型

英文的句子大部分都可以歸納為下面九種基本句型（basic sentence pattern）：

句型 1：　Noun＋Verb

　　　　　（Subject＋Verb）

　　　　　名詞＋動詞

　　　　　（主詞＋動詞）

句型 2：　Noun＋Verb＋Adverb or Prepositional Phrase

　　　　　（Subject＋Verb＋Complement）

　　　　　名詞＋動詞＋副詞或介詞片語

　　　　　（主詞＋動詞＋補語）

句型 3：　Noun＋Verb＋Noun

　　　　　（Subject＋Verb＋Direct Object）

　　　　　名詞＋動詞＋名詞

　　　　　（主詞＋動詞＋受詞）

句型 4：　Noun＋Verb＋Noun＋Noun

　　　　　（Subject＋Verb＋Indirect Object＋Direct Object）

　　　　　名詞＋動詞＋ 名詞＋名詞

　　　　　（主詞＋動詞＋間接受詞＋直接受詞）

句型 5 ： Noun＋Verb＋Noun or Adjective

（Subject＋Verb＋Object＋Object Complement）

名詞＋動詞＋名詞或形容詞

（主詞＋動詞＋受詞＋受詞補語）

句型 6 ： Noun＋Linking Verb＋Noun

（Subject＋Linking Verb＋Complement）

名詞＋連繫動詞＋名詞

（主詞＋連繫動詞＋補語）

句型 7 ： Noun＋Linking Verb＋Adjective, Adverb or Prepositional
Phrase

（Subject＋Linking Verb＋Complement）

名詞＋連繫動詞＋形容詞、副詞或介詞片語

（主詞＋連繫動詞＋補語）

句型 8 ： There＋Linking Verb＋Noun＋Adverb or Prepositional
Phrase

（There＋Linking verb＋Subject＋Complement）

There＋連繫動詞＋名詞＋副詞或介詞片語

（There＋連繫動詞＋主詞＋補語）

句型 9 ： It＋Linking Verb＋Adjective, Adverb, Noun, or
Prepositional Phrase

（It＋Linking Verb＋Complement）

It＋連繫動詞＋形容詞、副詞、名詞或介詞片語

（It＋連繫動詞＋補語）

現在我們將這九種句型作有系統的介紹，使讀者能有正確認識，從而奠定良好的寫作基礎。

句型 1： Noun＋Verb

（Subject＋Verb）

名詞＋動詞

（主詞＋動詞）

本句型僅僅含有名詞和動詞；沒有補語，也沒有受詞。本句型的動詞為不及物動詞（intransitive verb）。例如：

1. Fire burns.
2. Birds fly.
3. We all breathe.
4. The noise stopped.
5. Helen is singing.
6. The train has arrived.
7. The ship sailed.
8. It is raining.
9. The sun was shining.
10. The moon rose.

注意：在本句型及其他八個句型中，名詞相等詞及代名詞可取代名詞。

句型 2： Noun＋Verb＋Adverb or Prepositional Phrase

（Subject＋Verb＋Complement）

名詞＋動詞＋副詞或介詞片語

（主詞＋動詞＋補語）

本句型除了含有名詞和動詞以外，還含有副詞或介詞片語，此種副詞或介詞片語提供有關句中動詞的某種資料。本句型的動詞也是不及物動詞。例如：

1. Mr.Chang lives here.

2. Miss Wang works in a hospital.

3. She sings beautifully.

4. Mary went to the movies.

5. Her brother stayed at home.

6. We must study hard.

7. The sun rises in the east.

8. They did not go anywhere.

9. He will not come until ten.

10. I got up early.

句型 3： Noun＋Verb＋Noun

（Subject＋Verb＋Direct Object）

名詞＋動詞＋名詞

（主詞＋動詞＋受詞）

本句型的動詞為及物動詞（transitive verb），動詞前面的名詞為主詞，動詞後面的名詞為受詞。例如：

1. The boy cut his finger.

2. I do not like cold weather.

3. Mother is cooking dinner.

4. Father is reading a magazine.

5. Policemen help people.

6. Everyone likes Jane.

7. She smiled her thanks.

8. He made a fire.

9. They had a good time.

10. We will never compromise our principles.

句型 4： Noun＋Verb＋Noun＋Noun

（Subject＋Verb＋Indirect Object＋Direct Object）

名詞＋動詞＋ 名詞＋名詞

（主詞＋動詞＋間接受詞＋直接受詞）

本句型的動詞也是及物動詞，後面出現兩個名詞，第一個名詞是間接受詞，第二個名詞是直接受詞。間接受詞是及物動詞動作的接受者或產物，直接受詞指出及物動詞為他（它）做出動作的人（或物）。例如：

1. Mr.Wang teaches the students English.

2. He told them the truth.

3. I paid him a visit.

4. Mrs.Wang made Mary a skirt.

5. Peter gave Mary a birthday present.

6. Her father bought her a camera.

7. She wrote her mother a letter.

8. The policeman showed us the way.

9. John lent Jim fifty dollars.

10. Mother used to tell us stories.

本句型常用的動詞為 bring, cause, deny, do, envy, grant, guarantee, hand, leave, lend, make, offer, owe, pass, pay, play, rent, sell, send, show, spare, tell, throw 等。

以上各例句中的間接受詞均可改寫成介詞片語：

1. Mr.Wang teaches the students English.→

   Mr. Wang teaches English *to the students*.

2. He told them the truth.→

   He told the truth *to them*.

3. I paid him a visit.→

   I paid a visit *to him*.

4. Mrs.Wang made Mary a skirt.→

   Mrs. Wang made a skirt *for Mary*.

5. Peter gave Mary a birthday present.→

   Peter gave a birthday present *to Mary*.

6. Her father bought her a camera.→

   Her father bought a camera *for her*.

7. She wrote her mother a letter.→

   She wrote a letter *to her mother*.

8. The policeman showed us the way.→

   The policeman showed the way *to us*.

9. John lent Jim fifty dollars.→

   John lent fifty dollars *to Jim*.

10. Mother used to tell us stores.→

    Mother used to tell stories *to us*.

但有些動詞後面的間接受詞不能改寫成介詞片語。例如：

I envy Mary her long eyelashes.

We should spare him that humiliation.

以上兩句中的間接受詞不能改寫成介詞片語。這一類的動詞包括 spare, envy, cost, deny 等。

句型 5： Noun＋Verb＋Noun or Adjective

（Subject＋Verb＋Object＋Object Complement）

名詞＋動詞＋名詞或形容詞

（主詞＋動詞＋受詞＋受詞補語）

乍看起來，句型 5 和句型 4 很相似，細看起來，它們卻大不相同。在句型 4 中，動詞後面的兩個名詞是用做間接受詞和直接受詞，而且兩者所指的是不同的人或事物。在句型 5 中，動詞後面的第一個名詞是受詞，受詞後面的名詞或形容詞係用做受詞補語，而且兩者所指的是同一人或事物。例如：

1. That man called the scientist an expert.

2. The students thought the teacher strict.

3. The class elected David its president.

4. Studying keeps John busy.

5. The sunset made the sky red.

6. They believed him innocent.

7. Do you consider her honest?

8. I consider is a shame.

9. We proved him wrong.

10. Her singing made everyone happy.

句型 6： Noun＋Linking Verb＋Noun

（Subject＋Linking Verb＋Complement）

名詞＋連繫動詞＋名詞

（主詞＋連繫動詞＋補語）

　　本句型的動詞為連繫動詞，連繫動詞後面的名詞係用做主詞補語，對主詞加以說明。最常用的連繫動詞是動詞 be,但是 become，remain 等連繫動詞也適用於本句型。例如：

1. I am a student.

2. That man is a lawyer.

3. His father was a doctor.

4. Her parents are both teachers.

5. Asia is a continent.

6. China is an old country.

7. They are Americans.

8. Snow becomes water.

9. Mr. Chang will remain a soldier.

10. Man remained a hunter for thousands of years.

句型 7： Noun＋Linking Verb＋Adjective, Adverb or Prepositional
         Phrase
         （Subject＋Linking Verb＋Complement）
         名詞＋連繫動詞＋形容詞、副詞或介詞片語
         （主詞＋連繫動詞＋補語）

本句型的動詞主要是連繫動詞 be, remain, become,但也包括其他連繫動詞 appear, continue, feel, grow, seem, taste, turn 等。在本句型中，主詞補語是形容詞，但在動詞 be 及其他少數連繫動詞之後，也可以用表示地方的副詞（adverb of place）或做副詞用的介詞片語（adverbial prepositional phrase）。例如：

1.   That boy is intelligent.

2.   Robert seems stupid.

3.   The team grew tired.

4.   That situation appeared hopeless.

5.   That song remains popular.

6.   This dish tastes good.

7.   He has become rich.

8.   The leaves have turned red.

9.   The rug feels soft.

10. The plan proved useless.

11. My parents are here.

12. They can stay in this state for a month.

句型 8： There＋Linking Verb＋Noun＋Adverb or Prepositional Phrase

（There＋Linking verb＋Subject＋Complement）

There＋連繫動詞＋名詞＋副詞或介詞片語

（There＋連繫動詞＋主詞＋補語）

　　本句型以 there 開始，後面是接連繫動詞，there 並非主詞，真正的主詞是連繫動詞後面的名詞。連繫動詞的數完全以真正的主詞為準，一般說來，真正的主詞是單數，動詞就用單數，真正的主詞是複數，動詞就用複數。例如：

1. There is a spider under the bed.

2. There are ten boys on our team.

3. There is a book on the desk.

4. There is some money in the envelope.

5. There was an earthquake yesterday.

6. There were a few Americans at the party.

7. There is some ice cream in the refrigerator.

8. There was a movie on television.

9. There will be a test next week.

10. There will be a parade downtown.

11. There used to be a bridge here.

12. There were two children in the pond.

13. There seems (to be)no doubt about it.

14. There appeared to be no one who could answer our inquiries.

句型 9： It＋Linking Verb＋Adjective, Adverb, Noun, or

Prepositional Phrase

（It＋Linking Verb＋Complement）

It＋連繫動詞＋形容詞、副詞、名詞或介詞片語

（It＋連繫動詞＋補語）

本句型係以置於句首的 it 做主詞，用以表示日期、時間、天氣、距離等。例如：

1. It was March 8, 1983.

2. It was Tuesday.

3. It is quarter to nine.

4. It is early.

5. It is late.

6. It became lovely in spring.

7. It was a fine day.

8. It is cold today.

9. It is ten miles to the village.

10. It will be noisy there.

練 習 八

A. 以1, 2, 3, 4, 5, 6, 7, 8, 9代表九種基本句型，分別標示下列各句之句型。

例：This exercise is easy. (7)

The teacher told us an interesting story. (4)

It is ten to eleven. (9)

1. Her father is a banker.

2. The bus has arrived.

3. There will be an exam tomorrow.

4. It was raining hard.

5. Miss Chang teaches English.

6. The baby was crying.

7. The teacher asked Tom a question.

8. It was past midnight.

9. The committee appointed Jack treasurer.

10. She works in a bank.

11. It is her birthday.

12. That man is a dentist.

13. The children remained at home.

14. John is studying in the library.

15. The manager bought the secretary a computer.

16. There was a bundle of money in the box.

17. The story is very interesting.

18. The judge found him innocent.

19. The author wrote a new book.

20. That painting looks beautiful.

B.　將 A 部分的各句改為否定句。

　　例：That woman works in a department store.→

　　　　That woman does not work in a department store.

　　　　It is after two o'clock.→

　　　　It is not after two o'clock.

C.　將 A 部分的各句改為疑問句。

　　例：They elected John chairman.→

　　　　Did they elect John chairman?

　　　　It has been raining for more than a month.→

　　　　Has it been raining for more than a month?

第三章　句子的組合

下面是一個美國小學一年級生所寫的一篇作文：

OUR TRIP TO THE ZOO

We went to the zoo. We saw many animals. The animals were elephants, monkeys, and lions. We had our lunch at the zoo. We had soup, milk, bread, meat, and ice cream. After lunch we went to a big pool. Men were feeding big fish. We saw other boys and girls. We came home tired and happy.

就一個小學一年級生來說，這篇作文算是不錯了，因為句子的長度和表達的意思，大致都和小學一年級的程度稱合。但是在一個語文程度較高、思路更為複雜的中學生看起來，就會覺得這篇作文所包含的意思太簡單，句子太短，不大連貫，讀起來很單調。所以，一篇作文除了用簡單句以外，還應該用集合句或複合句。這一節將告訴你如何把簡單句組合成為集合句或複合句等比較長的句子。

第一節　主要子句的組合

主要子句可用對等連接詞 and, but, for, or, nor, so, yet 連接成集合句。例如：

1.　Bob moved to Taipei, *and* John moved to Tainan.

2.　Tom moved far away, *but* Jane stayed in her home town.

3.　Jim has saved money all year, *yet* he does not have enough for his vacation.

4.　Are you going to the party, *or* will you stay home?

5.　She does not write Japanese, *nor* does she speak it.

6.　That student failed, *for* he did not study hard.

7.　The dresses were cheap, *so* she bought all of them.

主要子句也可用 either...or, neither...nor, not only...but also 等相關連接詞（correlative conjunction）連接成集合句。例如：

Either you must improve your work *or* I will fire you.

Neither is he dependable, *nor* is he trustworthy.

Not only is she pretty, *but* she is *also* kind.

注意：如上面三個句子所示，在 neither, nor 或 not only 所引導的子句中，主詞和動詞的位置要顛倒。

主要子句也可用 however, therefore, otherwise, nevertheless, furthermore, hence, also, then, besides, accordingly, consequently, likewise, meanwhile 等連繫詞（connector）連接成集合句。例如：

Mary moved to Taichung; *however*, her mother stayed in Taipei.

He has broken the rules; *therefore*, he must be punished.

John is kind; *moreover*, he is generous.

Television can be entertaining; *furthermore*, it can be instructive.

She prepared her English lesson; *also*, she wrote her French composition.

He lives too far away to visit you often; *besides*, you are never at home.

The road was wet and slippery; *consequently*, there were many accidents.

The leaders settled the argument; *otherwise*, there would have been a war.

Mr. Wang was blind all his life; *nevertheless*, he had a successful career.

Tom requested permission to go home early; *accordingly*, his boss allowed him to leave the office at noon.

主要子句也可用 in fact, on the contrary, on the other hand, as a result, in the meantime等複合連繫詞（compound connector）連接成集合句。例如：

It is too late to finish the work; *in fact*, it is time to go home.

She is not a stupid girl; *on the contrary*, she is quite intelligent.

They may go to the movies; *on the other hand*, they may decide to visit their friend.

Jack worked hard all year; *as a result*, he made excellent progress.

He is going to France next year; *in the meantime*, he is learning French.

有時候，主要子句的組合既不用連接詞，也不用連繫詞，僅僅用分號。例如：

The sun was setting now; the shadows were long.

Lucy lives in Taipei; Larry lives in Keelung.

Cowards die many times before their deaths, the brave man dies but once.

練 習 九

用括弧內所提示的對等連接詞，將下列各組簡單句組合成集合句：

1. Prosperity makes friends.

    Adversity tries friends.（and）

2. Mr. White has lost his wallet.

    The whole family is upset.（and）

3. Grace has a new doll.

    She still prefers her old one.（but）

4. The performance was poor.

    The audience was enthusiastic.（but）

5. They stared late.

   They were delayed by some accident. (either...or)

6. Hurry up.

   You will miss the train. (or)

7. The Browns must be quite wealthy.

   They go abroad every year. (for)

8. You leave my house.

   I'll call the police. (either...or)

9. I decided to stop and have lunch.

   I was feeling quite hungry. (for)

10. I had a headache.

    I went to bed. (so)

11. The shops were closed.

    He couldn't get any bread. (so)

12. She's a clever girl.

    You can't help liking her. (yet)

第二節　名詞子句的組合

　　名詞子句是附屬子句的一種，具有名詞的功用。名詞子句可做句子的主詞，可做動詞、動名詞或介詞的受詞，可做補語，也可做同位語（appositive）。例如：

1.　*What he said* was meaningless.（主詞）

2.　I know *what his name is*.（動詞的受詞）

3.　Hearing *what he said*, she grew angry.（分詞的受詞）

4.　Peter asked her to read *what he had written*.（不定詞的受詞）

5.　Knowing *that she is here* is a comfort to me.（動名詞的受詞）

6.　She worried about *how ill he was*.（介詞的受詞）

7.　This is *what I think*.（主詞補語）

8.　One fact, *that he is hard-working*, cannot be disputed.（同位語）

　　名詞子句可用附屬連接詞、關係代名詞或關係形容詞 who, what, which, whom, whose, whoever, whichever, whatever, where, when, how, why, whether, that 引導，與主要子句組合成複合句。例如：

1.　She thought *that* Sam was coming.（附屬連接詞）

2.　She wondered *whether* he was coming.（附屬連接詞）

3.　She knew *what* he meant.（關係代名詞）

4.　She learned *who* said that.（關係代名詞）

5.　She wondered *which* course she should follow.（關係形容詞）

6.　She knew *whose* cat it was.（關係形容詞）

Ⅰ． 用做主詞的名詞子句

名詞子句既然具有名詞的功用，當然可以用做句子的主詞。例如：

1. *That he married her* isn't surprising.

2. *What is surprising* is that he stayed with her.

3. *Where he went from there* is not known.

4. *When the meeting will be held* has not been announced.

5. It is not known *where he had been.*

6. It's no wonder *that you can't sleep when you eat so much.*

7. It was not clear *who gave the order.*

8. It is remarkable *how he always gets out of trouble.*

9. It is believed *he entered by the back door.*

10. It's good *he returned safe and sound.*

用做主詞的名詞子句通常置於句首，如第一至四句；不過，在以 it 為形式主詞的句子中，則置於句尾，如第五至八句；在以 it 為形式主詞的句子中，引導名詞的連繫詞 that 有時可以省略，如第九至十句。

Ⅱ． 用做主詞補語的名詞子句

像名詞一樣，名詞子句可用做主詞補語。例如：

1. His problem was *how he should mention the matter.*

2. The important thing is *what a man does*, not *what he says.*

3. What I wonder is whether *Helen will be present.*

4. This is *where I found it.*

5. That is *what we want to know.*

6. We are *what we do.*

7. He is not *what he seems.*

8. It was probably *because his mother needed him.*

用做主詞補語的名詞子句通常置於句尾。如第八句所示，由附屬連接詞 because 所引導的子句有時也可用做主詞補語。

Ⅲ. 用做及物動詞之受詞的名詞子句

名詞子句多半用做及物動詞的直接受詞。例如：

1. I heard *that he flunked English.*

2. Do you know *whether he flunked English?*

3. Do you know *if he flunked English?*

4. He told her *how he caught the pheasant.*

5. He told her *where he caught the pheasant.*

6. We asked *when Nancy was going to perform.*

7. I wonder *why he didn't come to the party.*

8. I believe *what he said.*

9. Do you know *who that young lady is?*

10. Take *whatever you want.*

11. I know *he took the examination.*

12. I thought *you knew he passed the examination.*

用做動詞之受詞的名詞子句通常置於句尾。引導此種子句的連接詞以 that 最常見，但常被省略，如第十一至十二句。其他的附屬連接詞及

關係詞像 if, why, how, what 等，也常用以引導這種名詞子句。

Ⅳ. 用做介詞之受詞的名詞子句

名詞子句也常常用做介詞的受詞。例如：

1. She was worried about *whether she passed the English examination.*

2. They quarreled over *when the wedding date should be.*

3. There is some doubt as to *where the murder occurred.*

4. The men were paid according to *how much work they did.*

5. Give my regards to *whomever you see.*

6. He had to work with *what he had.*

7. She talked about *whatever came to his mind.*

用做介詞之受詞的名詞子句應置於介詞之後。由 that 和 if 所引導的名詞子句不能用做介詞的受詞。如第五至七句所示，由不定關係代名詞（indefinite relative pronoun）所引導的名詞子句常用做介詞的受詞。

練 習 十

A. 仔細閱讀下面一篇文章，選出其中含有名詞子句的句子，並按照順序把它們寫下來：

THE USES OF CARBON DATING

Scientists are interested in how people lived thousands of years ago. They want to find out what early peoples ate. Scientists used to study the cooking pots early peoples used and the bones of the animals they ate. But this method was not very accurate. Researchers have now developed a new method. They are studying the bones of early peoples. The carbon is the bones shows scientists what early peoples ate.

Carbon is an element found in all living things. It has two basic forms. More of one form is found in plants like corn. Less of this form is found in plants like manioc. Manioc is a root that grows in the wild. Early peoples could collect it to eat it. But to eat corn, early peoples had to stay in one place. They had to plant corn. The carbon type found in their bones shows whether the people ate manioc or corn. By knowing this, scientists can tell whether the people collected their food or grew it.

The carbon method also helps scientists find out what is in food today. For example, one company said its honey was pure. But a scientist

found two different kinds of carbon in it. The company had been mixing its honey with sugar cane juice!

B. 將下列各組簡單句組合成含有名詞子句的複合句。

例：The space shuttle could safely return even with damaged tiles.

They believed it.

→ They believed *that the space shuttle could safely return even with damaged tiles.*

Why did the car break down?

He is trying to find out.

→ He is trying to find out *why the car broke down.*

1. Where did he buy that pen?

I don't know.

2. Where did he find it?

Ask your brother.

3. How much did he pay for it?

I'll find out.

4. When are they coming?

She wants to know.

5. Why is Bob absent?

She will explain.

6. When will they arrive?

   I have no idea.

7. Where have they gone?

   Nobody knows.

8. Criticism often hurts others.

   Everyone knows it.

9. It will be resented.

   You showed your superiority.

10. You are right.

    That fact does not matter.

11. Poetry is difficult for some readers.

    It is fact.

12. Most poetry must be read slowly.

    This is true.

第三節　間接引語

　　把一個人所說的話完全不加更改地照樣引述出來，叫做直接引語（direct speech）。不把一個人所說的話完全照樣加以引述，而把那句話間接地敘述出來，叫做間接引語（indirect speech）。在下面十二組句子中，各組的第一句均為直接引語，各組的第二句均為間接引語：

1. "I am very angry," he said.

   He said that he was very angry.

2. "I'll behave myself," he promised.

   He promised that he'd behave himself.

3. "I live here," he explained.

   He explained that he lived there.

4. "I am tired," she complained.

   She complained that she was tired.

5. "The exhibition finished last week," explained Jane.

   Jane explained that the exhibition had finished the preceding week.

6. "I've won the match already!" exclaimed our friend.

   Our friend exclaimed that he had won the match already.

7. "The whole house had been ruined," said the storyteller.

   The storyteller said that the whole house had been ruined.

8. "You are very kind," she said to me.

   She told me that I was very kind.

9. "Are you ready yet?" asked Joan.

   Joan asked me whether I was ready yet.

10. "When will the plane leave?" I wondered.

    I wondered when the plane would leave.

11. "What are you doing?" she asked.

    She asked me what I was doing.

12. "How brave you are!" Mary told him.

    Mary told him how brave he was.

　　在間接引語中，所引述的別人的話多置於附屬子句中，並用 that 來引導那個附屬子句，如第一至八組句子。

　　從直接引語改為間接引語時，間接引語中的人稱代名詞應針對直接引語中的人稱代名詞作適當的改變。如第一、二、三、四、六組句子所示，直接引語中的第一人稱代名詞在間接引語中應該改為第三人稱。如第八、九、十一、十二組句子所示，直接引語中的第二人稱代名詞在間接引語中應該改為第一人稱或第三人稱。

　　有的時候，直接引語中的 this 在間接引語中要改為 that；these 要改為 those；here 要改為 there，如第三組句子；last week 要改為 the preceding week，如第五組句子；next week 要改為 the following week；yesterday 要改為 the previous day；tomorrow 要改為 the following day。

　　不過，從直接引語改為間接引語時，最重要的還是動詞時態的變化。如果引導間接引語的動詞（reporting verb）（也就是主要子句的動詞）是過去式，無論直接引語中的動詞是什麼時態，間接引語（也就是附屬子句）中的動詞都應該分別改為過去式或過去完成式，如第

一至十二組句子。從直接引語改為間接引語時，如果主要子句的動詞是過去式，有時動詞時態的變化，可綜合如下：

直接引語	間接引語
(1)現在式	過去式
(2)過去式	
(3)現在完成式	過去完成式
(4)過去完成式	

如第十至十一組句子所示，從直接問句（direct question）改成間接問句（indirect question）時，間接問句中的代名詞和動詞等也應該作適當的改變。要特別注意的是，間接問句不再用疑問句的詞序，而應該用敘述句的詞序，也就是「（疑問詞）＋主詞＋動詞」的詞序。間接問句的末尾不用問號。

如第九組句子所示，直接問句若為〔是或不〕問句，間接問句中的附屬子句應該用 whether 或 if 來引導。

練 習 十 一

將下列各直接引語改成間接引語。

例："I am glad I can visit Taiwan," Mr. Smith said.

Mr. Smith said that he was glad he could visit Taiwan.

"Where's the house located?" he asked.

He asked where the house was located.

"Was my son hurt?" asked the old woman.

The old woman asked whether her son was hurt.

1. "I want to help people of my country," he said.

2. "A formal announcement will be made next week," he explained.

3. "The poor man has been here almost a year," he said.

4. "That's why I bought this old record," explained Helen.

5. "We like to wear old-fashioned clothes." said Mary.

6. "This is a very special show," he explained.

7. "My husband wants to move here," she said.

8. "It takes me half a year to earn that much money," he complained.

9. "It's the biggest race of the racing season," said Ralph.

10. "The waves look pretty rough today!" Betty exclaimed.

11. "Where is my bicycle?" John asked.

12. "Have you seen my brother?" asked Jim.

13. "What did John buy yesterday?" Tom asked.

14. "Have you finished your work?" he asked.

15. "Are you going to the movies?" she asked me.

16. "Is the bus coming?" Peter said to me.

17. "Where did you lose your key?" he asked.

18. "How much will the watch cost?" asked David.

19. "When did he last write to you?" she asked.

20. "Why is she crying?" he asked.

第四節　形容詞子句的組合

形容詞子句也是附屬子句的一種，具有形容詞的功用，可用來形容名詞或代名詞。例如：

1.　I want to see the man *who sold a car to Mr. Wang*.

2.　Let me show you the man *whom you want to see*.

3.　This is the man *whose car was sold to Mr. Wang*.

4.　The car *which is parked in front of the building* belongs to Mr. Wang.

5.　The car *that Mr. Wang bought* is a very good one.

6.　This is the place *where Mr. Wang's car was made*.

7.　This is the year *when Mr. Wang's car was made*.

8.　Do you know the reason *why Mr. Wang bought the car*?

形容詞子句通常是用關係代名詞 who, whom, whose, which, that 來引導，如第一至五句；有時也用關係副詞 where, when, why 來引導，如第六至八句。關係代名詞 who 用以指人，which 用以指事物，that 用以指人或事物。所以，在第一、四兩句中，who 和 which 可以跟 that 通用；在第五句中，that 可以跟 which 通用。

I. 限制性子句與非限制性子句

形容詞子句分為限制性子句（restrictive）和非限制性子句（nonrestrictive）。限制性子句用來指明它所形容的名詞或代名詞，這個形容詞子句如果被省略，句子的意思就會改變或不清楚；限制性子

句與其所形容的名詞或代名詞之間不能加逗號。非限制性子句只是附帶說明它所形容的名詞,即使被省略,也不會改變句子的意思或使句子變得不清楚;非限制性子句與其所形容的名詞之間要用逗號分開。現在請比較下面兩句:

My brother *who lives in Taichung* is coming to visit me.

My brother, *who lives in Taichung*, is coming to visit me.

前面一句的意思是「我那個住在台中的兄弟將要來看我」,說這句話的人還有別的兄弟住在別的地方;所以,前面一句的形容詞子句是限制性子句,指明哪一個兄弟要去看他。後面一句的意思是「我的兄弟將要來看我,他住在台中」,說這句話的人表示他只有這麼一個兄弟;所以後面一句裡的形容詞子句是非限制性子句,附帶說明他的兄弟住在台中。

II.　關係詞的省略

限制性子句的關係詞如為該子句的主詞,則不能省略,如下面第一句;限制性子句的關係詞如非該子句主詞,則可以省略,如下面第二至五句。非限制性子句的關係詞不能省略,如下面第六、七兩句:

1. The car *which is parked in front of the building* belongs to Mr. Wang.

2. The car (*that*) *Mr. Wang bought* is a very good one.

3. This is the place (*where*) *Mr. Wang's car was made*.

4. This is the year (*when*) *Mr. Wang's car was made*.

5. Do you know the reason (*why*) *Mr. Wang bought the car?*

6. Mr. Wang, *who bought the car*, is a banker.

7. Mr. Wang, *whom we all respect,* is a kind man.

練 習 十 二

A. 仔細閱讀下面一篇文章，選出其中含有形容詞子句的句子，並按照順序把它們寫下來：

MAKING AN ANIMATED FILM

Animation is the technique of making motion-picture cartoons from a series of drawings. The range of animation techniques is quite broad. However, the basic form of animation is the outlined figure that moves against an outlined background. The first step in making an animated movie is finding a story. Many animated films are made for children and are based on fairy tales and children's books. After a story has been decided upon, an artist-writer prepares a storyboard, which serves as the film's script. The storyboard is like a giant comic strip. It consists of rough sketches that show the action of the story, with the dialogue printed with

each sketch.

After the director and other key personnel approve the storyboard, the music and dialogue are recorded. The composer carefully follows the storyboard to make sure the music matches each sequence of the action.

Then layout artists, working with the director, determine what settings will be drawn, how each character will act and look, and how the story can best be broken into scenes. After these decisions have been made, the layout artists prepare drawings to guide the other artists, who will actually draw each scene.

B. 用 who, whom, whose, which 或 that 將下列各組簡單句組合成含形容詞子句的複合句。

例：The boy found it.

He is my cousin.

The boy *who found it* is my cousin.

1. He has lost the key.

The key fits all the doors.

2. That is the man.

I bought the watch from that man.

3. That pitcher played last night.

    He was not very good.

4. I know the girl.

    Her father owns the restaurant.

5. A woman saw the accident.

    Do you know the woman's name?

6. The bridge crosses the river near the village.

    It is definitely unsafe.

7. They caught a thief.

    He has confessed.

8. I want to see the man.

    He is in charge of production.

9. I have just been speaking to a man.

    His dog bit Bob yesterday.

10. The fire started at six o'clock.

    It lasted for three hours.

C. 用 in which, from which, from whom, to whom 等將下列各組簡單
    句組合成含形容詞子句的複合句。

    例：We watched the game.

      John scored a home run in it.

      We watched the game *in which John scored a home run.*

      That is the boy.

I bought this camera from him.

That is the boy *from whom I bought this camera.*

I don't know the name of the man.

I spoke to him.

I don't know the name of the man *to whom I spoke.*

1. That is the taxi.

    We came in it.

2. There is a shop.

    I bought my watch from it.

3. David was the boy.

    I borrowed a book from him.

4. Those are the men.

    I sold the oranges to them.

5. Do you know the girl?

    Helen spoke to her.

6. That is the window.

    He jumped from that window.

7. This is the door.

    The two men escaped through this door.

8. The police have found the knife.

    He was killed with it.

9. That is the boy.

    He was playing with her.

10. The hotel was both cheap and comfortable.

   We stayed at the hot.

D. 用 who, whose, whom, which, that, when, where 或 why 將下列各組
   簡單句組合成含形容詞子句的複合句。

   例：Do you recognize the man?

      You met him at the party.

      Do you recognize the man *that you met at the party*?

      There is my friend.

      You have heard about him.

      There is my friend *whom you have heard about*.

      Here is the place.

      Few people come here.

      Here is a place *where few people come*.

1. Do you see the lady?

   I ate lunch with her yesterday.

2. I have a friend.

   He can help you.

3. The dog was friendly.

   He wagged his tail.

4. The house is comfortable.

   He lives there.

5. Those oranges were very sweet.

   We ate four of them.

6. The sun was shining.

   I walked in the garden.

7. You took a vacation last week.

   Was it pleasant?

8. She didn't remember the man's name.

   It was difficult to pronounce.

9. I know a woman.

   She lives on a boat.

10. Have you seen the club?

    It has a large swimming pool.

第五節　副詞子句的組合

副詞子句也是附屬子句的一種，具有副詞的功用，可用來修飾動詞、準動詞、形容詞、副詞或另一子句。例如：

John studies *as all his brothers before him have studied.*（修飾動詞）

Flying *until he was out of gas*, Charles crashed.（修飾準動詞）

His reply was quicker *than it should have been.*（修飾形容詞）

Winter came earlier *than it ever did before.*（修飾副詞）

As it turned out, Tom had some money with him.（修飾主要子句）

副詞子句分為表示時間、地方、情形或方式、程度、結果、目的、原因、條件、讓步等子句。

Ⅰ. 表示時間的副詞子句

像表示時間的副詞一樣，表示時間的副詞子句（adverb clauses of time）可以回答用 when 開始的問句。常用的連接詞有 when, whenever, before, after, until, since, once, now that, as soon as。例如：

Abraham Lincoln maintained great interest in legal studies *when he was President.*

He read law books *whenever he had the chance.*

He even read *while he conducted cabinet meetings.*

He had wanted to be a lawyer *since he was a young boy.*

He worked as a lawyer *after he finished his education.*

He was a member of the legislature of his state *before he became President.*

He maintained his interest in law *until he was assassinated.*

We will better appreciate Lincoln the lawyer *when we study his legal opinion.*

Ⅱ. 表示地方的副詞子句

像表示地方的副詞一樣，表示地方的副詞子句（adverb clauses of place）可以回答用 where 開始的問句。常用的連接詞為 where 和 wherever。例如：

She has always lived *where she was born.*

Wherever you go, I will follow you.

Ⅲ. 表示情形或方式的副詞子句

表示情形或方式的副詞子句（adverb clauses of manner）可以回答用 how 開始的問句。主要的連接詞為 as, as if, as though, in that。例如：

I write *as I please.*

Jim acted *as if he were frightened.*

David nodded quietly, *as though he understood every word.*

Bill disappointed his mother *in that he didn't write home very often.*

IV. 表示程度的副詞子句

表示程度的副詞子句（adverb clauses of degree）可以回答用 how much, how little, how many 等開始的問句。主要的連接詞為 as...as, so...as 和 than。例如：

She is almost *as* naughty *as her brother is.*

She does not talk *so* loudly *as her daughter does.*

He is older *than I am.*

V. 表示結果的副詞子句

表示結果的副詞子句（adverb clauses of result）說明由於主要子句中的行動或狀態，因而發生或可能發生甚麼事情。主要的連接詞為 so that, so...that, such...that。例如：

It rained hard all day, *so that we got nothing more done in the garden.*

The smaller puppy had *such a cute smile that we couldn't help liking him.*

The novel was *so* interesting *that I finished reading it in one evening.*

It was *such* an interesting novel *that I finished reading it in one evening.*

VI. 表示目的的副詞子句

表示目的的副詞子句（adverb clauses of purpose）說明主要動詞的行動所具有的目的。常見的連接詞為 in order that, so, so that 及 lest。例如：

School was closed early *in order that the children might get home ahead of the storm.*

Jack put a new lock on the garage *so no one would steal his car.*

They pushed their way to the front of the hall *so that they could see the performance clearly.*

I watered the lawn *so that it would grow.*

Tom slammed the door *so that his mother would know he was home.*

VII. 表示原因的副詞子句

表示原因的副詞子句（adverb clauses of cause）說明主要子句的行動的原因或理由。最常見的連接詞為 because, since, as。例如：

Don't scamp your work *because you are pressed for time.*

As it's raining, you'd better take a taxi.

Since we have no money, we can't buy it.

由 that 引導的副詞子句常用來修飾形容詞，這種子句也可以視為表示原因的副詞子句。例如：

I am sorry *that you feel that way.*

We are so glad *that you can come.*

We were pleased *that it stopped raining.*

在修飾形容詞的副詞子句中，連接詞常常省略。例如：

We are glad *you can come.*

Fred feels confident *he will pass the examination.*

VIII. 表示條件的副詞子句

表示條件的副詞子句（adverb clauses of condition）提供某種情況，在此種情況下，主要子句的陳述將會實現，或某種行動將會發生。主要的連接詞為 if, unless, provided that, so long as。例如：

I'll drop in *if I have time*.

If you treat her kindly, she'll do anything for you.

He will not sign the contract *unless it is satisfactory*.

Unless the strike has been called off, there will be no trains tomorrow.

We'll have plenty of sandwiches, *provided that no uninvited guests turn up*.

You can go out, *so long as you promise to be back before 11 o'clock*.

If it was to rain, we should get wet.

If John were here, we would learn the truth.

表示條件的副詞子句置於句首，而且以（助）動詞 should 或 were 引導時，連接詞通常省略。例如：

Should anything happen to me, give this envelope to Helen.

Were it not for her young son, Mrs. Wang could take a full-time job.

IX. 表示讓步的副詞子句

表示讓步的副詞子句（adverb clauses of concession）說明與主要子句內容相反的事物，但並不否認主要子句內容的正確性。主要的連接詞為 although, though, even if／though, while 及 whereas。例如：

Mr. Wang is generous *although he is poor*.

Though it's hard work, she enjoys it.

Even if you don't like beer, try a glass of this!

They managed to survive, *even though they were three days without water*.

While I understand what you say, I can't agree with you.

Whereas Peter had numerous enemies, his brother was loved by everyone.

還有一種常見的句子，其中表示讓步的連接詞跟在附屬子句的主詞補語後面。例如：

Young though he is, Mr. Smith holds a responsible position in his firm.

Tired as he was, John was determined to drive home that night.

練 習 十 三

A. 仔細閱讀下面一篇文章，選出其中含有副詞子句的句子，按照順序寫下來，並說明每一個副詞子句的用法：

THE DOG'S SENSES

The dog's most developed sense is its sense of smell. The area in a dog's brain concerned with smell is comparatively much larger than that in a

man's brain. Practical scents—smells that identify other animals—are of the greatest interest to a dog. When a dog smells an interesting or an unusual scent, it usually rapidly sniffs the air. This allows more air to enter its nose, which has a very sensitive lining.

Dogs also have an acute sense of hearing. They can hear sounds up to 90,000 cycles per second. By comparison, an adult man can hear sounds only up to 20,000 cycles per second. Dogs can also clearly distinguish the character of sounds. Thus many pet dogs can hear the family car approaching long before the human ear detects any sound at all.

Many dogs do not have good eyesight. If an object has no smell and is not moving, a dog may not even notice it. Most hunting dogs do not see their prey until it moves. And quite interesting is the fact that all dogs are color blind.

Very little is known about a dog's sense of taste. However, tests have shown that dogs can identify a flavor with 97.8% accuracy.

B. 用括弧內的連接詞將各組簡單句組合成含有副詞子句的複合句。

例：John will attend a technical college.

He wants to be an engineer.（so that）

John will attend a tachnical college *so that he can be an engineer.*

1. John is only sixteen.

   He has already entered a university.（although）

2. He studied hard in high school.

   He wanted to be accepted by a good university.（because）

3. He always conducted himself properly.

   He was older than his years.（as if）

4. His family lived a long way from a university.

   He had to move to a strange city.（since）

5. He reached the university.

   Classes had not yet started.（when）

6. He was searching for a place to live.

   He met a foreign student.（while）

7. The two boys became acquainted.

   They decided to share a room.（after）

8. The two boys could live with little money.

   They decided to find an inexpensive place to live.（so that）

9. They planned their expenditures carefully.

    They would not have enough money.（unless）

10. They looked for a room.

    The two friends consulted the Dean.（before）

C. 用 although 引導一個副詞子句，將各組簡單句組合成複合句。

    例：I did not turn on the fan.

    I was hot.（although）

    Although I was hot, I did not turn on the fan.

1. The hill was steep.

    I rode up it.

2. We played basketball.

    It was very hot.

3. They played football.

    It was raining hard.

4. The watch was very expensive.

    He bought it.

5. She was late.

    She did not hurry up.

6. This watch is not accurate.

    I paid five thousand dollars for it.

7. I invited them.

    They did not come.

8. We managed to get to school.

   The road was flooded.

D. 將下列各組簡單句組合成含副詞子句的複合句，用 when 或 after 取代各句中的斜體字，副詞子句中的動詞一律用完成式。

   例：The film finished.

   Then we went home.

   When the film had finished, we went home.

   We left Taipei.

   A few hours *later* we reached Tainan.

   We reached Tainan a few hours *after we had left Taipei*.

1. She dug a hole.

   Then she buried the trash.

2. We finished playing football.

   Then Then we had an iced drink.

3. The plane landed safely.

   Most of the passengers got off.

4. She washed the fruit.

   Then she gave us some.

5. John washed the car.

   Jim and I dried it.

6. She hung out the clothes.

   A few minutes *later* it began to rain.

7. We left Taiwan.

    Three days *later* we arrived in Singapore.

8. He finished repairing the wall.

    He had a rest.

9. She finished the letter.

    She mailed it.

10. I turned off the tap.

    I started to repair the washing machine.

第六節　綜合組句

　　所謂綜合組句（synthesis），就是根據各簡單句所含各項事實之間的合理關係，以各種不同的方式把它們組合成為比較複雜的句子。我們現在來考慮一下下面三個句子所含的各項事實：

1.　John used to go to school.

2.　He carried a schoolbag.

3.　This schoolbag contained his homework.

我們可以把這三個句子組合成為一個比較複雜的句子：

When John went to school, he carried a schoolbag containing his homework.

在這個句子裡，he carried a schoolbag 被視為主要的事實；其他部分被視為次要的事實，說明帶書包的時間和書包裡所裝的東西。這兩項次要的事實是分別用附屬子句和片語表達出來的。

　　上面三個簡單句也可以用另一種方式組合成為一個比較複雜的句子：

John used to go to school carrying a schoolbag which contained his homework.

在這個句子裡，John used to go to school 被視為主要的事實；其他部分被視為次要的事實，分別以附屬子句和片語來表達。

　　所以，把任何一組句子所含各項事實併在一個句子裡表達出來，其方式都不止一種，往往有好幾種。作文的人首先要決定哪一項是主要的事實，哪幾項是次要的事實，然後才開始造句。

再以下面一組的句子所含各項事實為例：

1. The murderer was well acquainted with the methods of the police.

2. He had fallen into their hands before.

3. He continued to underrate their efficiency.

4. He hid in a small hotel.

5. He was soon discovered.

這組句子所含的各項事實顯然都是同性質的，可以用一個句子表達如下：

Though the murderer, having fallen into the hands of the police before, was well acquainted with their methods, he continued to underrate their efficiency, for he hid in a small hotel and was soon discovered.

練 習 十 四

將下列每組句子組合成為一個較長的句子。

例：The children were playing happily.

They lost all track of time.

They were late for dinner.

The children were playing so happily that they lost all track of time and were late for dinner.

1. The river overflowed its banks.

    It flooded the farmer's rice fields.

    The farmer had just planted his rice fields.

2. Sue was doing poorly in math.

    She hired a tutor.

    He was a college student majoring in math.

3. Jogging is a form of exercise.

    It is popular all over the world.

    It is very good for one's health.

4. Energy conservation is very important.

    It can save us money.

    The world's natural resources are limited.

5. She was thinking about her boyfriend.

    She hadn't heard from him for several days.

    She decided to write him a letter.

6. My elder brother is a college student.

    He does his homework at night.

    He concentrates intently on what he does.

    I enter his room.

    He doesn't notice me.

7. Mike was awakened by a strange noise.

    He leaped out of bed.

    He went to investigate.

He discovered a burglar.

The burglar was trying to climb over the wall.

8. John and Mary attended the concert.

   It was held at the Dr. Sun Yat-sen Memorial Hall.

   They enjoyed all of the songs.

   Their favorite song was " Killing Me Softly."

   It was sung at the end of the show.

9. Allen felt a little hungry one evening.

   He went out to the local noodle stand.

   He ran into an old friend.

   He hadn't seen him for several months.

   He didn't return home until midnight.

10. Jack is my neighbor.

    He is a businessman.

    He works hard all week.

    He relaxes on Sunday.

    His favorite pastime is fishing.

11. The store was built by my brother.

    It is a small store.

    I cannot sell many things in it.

    There is not enough room for the customers.

12. There was a pretty girl living in a village.

    She was very kind to her neighbors.

The village was called Ta Nan.

The girl's name was May.

Her neighbors liked her very much because of her kindness.

13. The hall was crowded.

There were many men and women.

Some were standing.

Some were sitting.

14. The sun set.

The sky grew cloudy.

The lightning flashed.

The thunder rumbled.

Then it rained.

He hurried home.

15. Last night I had a nightmare.

It was a dreadful one.

It did not last long.

I can still remember it.

16. He was driving very fast.

He was in a hurry.

He nearly knocked down an old woman.

She was crossing the road.

17. We reached the island.

We landed.

We could not see anybody.

There were many birds.

They made a lot of noise.

We went near them.

They flew away.

18. She takes care of her family very well.

   She never loses her temper.

   She works very hard.

19. At ten o'clock the weather was cold.

   The sky was blue.

   The moon shone brightly.

20. We could see colorful fish swimming in the water.

   The water was crystal clear.

21. My aunt lives in Taichung.

   She came to see us.

   She came last week.

22. Wc were walking for most of the afternoon.

   We were hungry.

   We were walking through fields and along trails.

   We did not talk to each other.

23. Helen is a lovely girl.

   She is now only six years old.

   Her mother loves her very much.

She is the youngest child in the family.

24. He took the culprits to the police station.

It was on Ho-ping East Road.

There was a police officer there.

The police officer thanked him very much.

25. She asked him something.

She wanted to know how much the camera was.

He replied to her.

He said it cost two thousand dollars.

第四章　怎樣寫出好句子

一個句子除了要語法正確以外，還得清晰、簡練、富有意義。本章將告訴你怎樣使句子清晰而有效，怎樣避免造句常犯的錯誤，怎樣使句子有變化，怎樣加強句子的語氣。

第一節　怎樣使句子清晰而有效

我們對於句子的基本要求，是要它很清晰而有效地把意思表達出來。欲求達到這個目的，必須做到下列兩點：

Ⅰ．保持句子的統一性（unity）

一個句子無論多麼長多麼複雜，只要它很清晰地表達一個中心的意思，使其他附帶的意思居於次要地位，或者把它們去掉，這個句子就可以說是統一的。

下面這四個句子缺少統一性：

1. The *Central Daily News* is my favorite newspaper, and I live in Taipei.
2. Mr.Wang built our new house, and it is a frame house.
3. The boy dancing with my sister is Tom Chang, and he is my best friend.
4. The girl was very pretty, but she covered her face with a large veil.

上面的每個句子都包含兩個同樣重要的意思，讀者讀了會感到困惑，因為他的心思被迫同時朝著兩個方向前進。

怎樣改進這些句子呢？你可以把第一句分成兩個句子，並且為了邏輯的關係，把順序顛倒一下，成為下列的兩個句子：

I live in Taipei.

The *Central Daily News* is my favorite newspaper.

現在每個句子都具有統一性了。

在第二句和第三句裡，你可以使不重要的意思居於次要的地位：

Mr. Wang built our new house, a frame house.

The boy dancing with my sister is Tom Chang, my best friend.

至於第四句，為了表達確切的意思，你可以添加一點東西，成為下列的句子：

The girl was very pretty, but no one knew it because she covered her face with a large veil.

由上面這些例子，我們可以看出，為了使句子具有統一性，最好能做到下列各點：

1.　把不相關聯的陳述分別放在單獨的句子裡面。

2.　使不重要的陳述居於次要地位。

3.　填補句子所表現的意思方面的漏洞。

Ⅱ.　保持句子的連貫性（coherence）

如果把一個句子的各部分按照適當的順序安排得很緊湊，給人一種清晰明確的觀念，不會引起誤解，這個句子就是連貫的。

句子不連貫，往往是由於疏忽造成的，作文的人沒有把句子的中心意思想通，以致在半途迷失方向，未能把整個意思清晰而正確地表達出來。

為了保持句子的連貫性，要注意下列兩項基本的要求：

（一）　**不要把修飾語放錯位置**。有些單字，如 only, almost, just, ever, never 和 nearly 之類，如果放錯位置，會破壞全句的意思。這些字通常都要放在它們所修飾的字的前面；如果句子的結構不容許這樣做，也要設法把那個修飾語究竟修飾哪一個字交代清楚。例如：

1. 錯：　She was only ill on Friday, and well enough for the dance Saturday night.

　　對：　She was ill only on Friday, and well enough for the dance Saturday night.

2. 錯：　Prosperity is not only the result of knowing how to make money, but also of knowing how to save it.

　　對：　Prosperity is the result not only of knowing how to make money but also of knowing how to save it.

介詞片語（prepositional phrase）通常要緊接著放在它所修飾的字的後面：

　　錯：　Tom waited for his friend who lived in Taichung at the Taipei Railway Station.

　　對：　Tom waited at the Taipei Railway Station for his friend who lived in Taichung.

(二)　**代名詞的先行詞（antecedent）要交代清楚**。例如下列各組第一句的意思便是含糊不清的：

1.　含糊：　We took up the rugs in both rooms and cleaned them thoroughly for the party.

　　清晰：　We took up the rugs and cleaned both rooms for the party.

2.　含糊：　One of the girls had brought her younger sister, but she didn't have much fun on the trip.

　　清晰：　One of the girls, who had brought her younger sister, didn't have much fun on the trip.

　　清晰：　One of the girls had brought her younger sister, but the little girl didn't have much fun on the trip.

練 習 十 五

改正下列各句：

1.　Chaucer was born in London, probably about 1340, and he was the first great English poet.

2.　The children's lunches are all packed, and they're ready to go.

3.　His parents were negligent; they allowed the boy to act as he pleased.

4.　She has almost won all the prizes.

5.　He nearly enjoys every motion picture he sees.

6. I can only hear a low mumble of voices.

7. She saw a beautiful dress in the shop window of black lace.

8. Gloria's mother studied nursing as a girl, and now she herself is thinking of becoming one.

9. Bruce told my brother that he wasn't eligible.

10. Stevens,the writer, died after an automobile accident in the hospital.

第二節　怎樣避免造句常犯的錯誤

Ⅰ．避免造出不合習慣語法的句子

　　我們中國人學英文，常會造出不合習慣語法（unidiomatic）的句子來。下面是一些例子，各組的第一句均不合習慣語法，學寫英文作文的人應該儘量避免造這種錯誤的句子；各組的第二句是比較正確的說法，可供參考。

1.　* The whole city likes a dead one.

　　The whole city is like a dead one.

2.　* Although English is not my specialty, but I do my best to help my students.

　　Although English is not my specialty, I will do my best to help my students.

3.　* I am looking forward to receive your letter.

　　I am looking forward to receiving your letter.

4.　* Perhaps the poor men are happier than the rich one.

　　Perhaps the poor are happier than the rich.

5.　* First you must decide where are you going.

　　First you must decide where you are going.

6.　* You can see the farmers work in the field hardly.

　　You can see the farmers working hard in the field.

7.   * A beautiful highway rounds the lake.

There is a beautiful highway round the lake.

8.   * There were many farmers to work under the mountain.

There were many farmers working at the foot of the mountain.

9.   * They very love me and I respect them also.

They love me very much and I respect them, too.

10.   * I enjoy listening music and fishing.

I enjoy fishing and listening to music.

11.   * I am interesting in mountain climbing.

I am interested in mountain climbing.

12.   * I can see many books in a year.

I can read many books in a year.

13.   * All these words are my teacher's advices.

All these words are my teacher's advice.

14.   * We can see how lovely girl she is.

We can see what a lovely girl she is.

15.   * I live in the dormitory, with six boys live together in one room.

I live in the dormitory, with six boys living together in one room.

16.   * Besides, she is a good-tempered girl, everything can't irritate her.

Besides, she is such a good-tempered girl that nothing can irritate her.

17.　＊Now it know I was impossible to be a doctor.

　　　Now I know I was impossible for me to be a doctor.

18.　＊She is a good cooker, too.

　　　She is a good cook, too.

19.　＊Probably no other American can get more honor than him.

　　　Probably no other American can get more honor than he.

20.　＊He was thirteen, his parents were both died.

　　　He was thirteen, and both of his parents were dead.

II. 避免使用沒有適當連接詞的句子

　　所謂沒有適當連接詞的句子（run-on sentence）就是指含有好幾個子句，但各子句之間沒有適當的連接詞，僅有逗號連接的句子。例如：

　　The author associated with a pretty girl, the girl who was so lovely attracted him, she told him what her brother was, beautiful, handsome, diligent in his studies and so on, from her shining eyes, we could know how she loved him.

上面這個句子是個典型的沒有適當連接詞的句子，而且語法有誤，措詞不妥。我們可以把它分成幾個較短但意思較清楚的句子：

　　The author became acquainted with a pretty girl who was so lovely that he was attracted to her. She told him that her brother was handsome and diligent in his studies. From her shining eyes, he knew how much she loved her brother.

除了把這種句子分成幾個較短的句子以外，也可用分號或連接詞把各子句連接起來。例如：

>*I used to enjoy detective stories, now I am tired of them.

>I used to enjoy detective stories; now I am tired of them.

Ⅲ. 避免使用無所依歸的準動詞

準動詞（verbals）包含分詞（participles）、動名詞（gerunds）和不定詞（infinitives），它們仍具有動詞的性質，所以必有其做出動作的人或物。準動詞置於句首時，如果後面不指明做出動作的人或物，便會使句子的意思不清楚，這種準動詞，就叫做無所依歸的準動詞（dangling verbals）。例如：

1. *Having read Poe, the stories of O. Henry interested her.

   Having read Poe, she became interested in O. Henry's stories.

2. *In reading them, one difference could be found.

   In reading them, she found one difference.

3. *To surprise his readers, unexpected endings are used.

   To surprise his readers, O. Henry uses unexpected endings.

在上面三組句子中，每一組的第一句均含有無所依歸的準動詞。第一組中的分詞片語 Having read Poe 不應該修飾 the stories，而應該修飾做出動作者 she。第二組中含有動名詞的介詞片語所要修飾的也應該是做出動作者 she，而不是 one difference。第三組中的不定詞片語應該修飾做出動作者 O. Henry，不應該修飾unexpected endings。寫英文作文時，應該避免寫出這種含有無所依歸的準動詞的句子。

練 習 十 六

改正下列各句，務使各分詞有所依歸。

例：*Running faster than ever, records were broken.

Running faster than ever, the runners broke records.

1. Having drunk our sodas, the train left as we reached the platform.

2. After listening to the speaker for a few minutes, my thoughts began to wander.

3. Covered with a mantle of snow, we saw the forest.

4. Rising to face his audience, every word of Jack's prepared speech left his mind.

5. By smiling cheerfully, a gloomy mood can often be chased away.

6. While fishing today, my hook was tangled in a mass of seaweed.

7. Arriving at Taipei, the city was so large that he was frightened.

8. Cooled by air conditioning, you could make this room quite comfortable.

9. Seeing Jenny at the station, the surprise was overwhelming.

10. After driving several miles on the highway, the sign showed that we were going in the wrong direction.

練　習　十　七

A.　用分詞片語組合下列各組句子，在句首的分詞片語後面要用一個逗號。

　　例：Bob turned to the right.

　　　　He saw a white horse.

　　　　Turning to the right, Bob saw a white horse.

　　1.　Mary laughed gaily.

　　　　She turned away.

　　2.　Tom shook his fist at me.

　　　　He walked back to the car.

　　3.　The child was abandoned by every one.

　　　　He was weeping bitterly.

　　4.　The thief watched his chance.

　　　　He suddenly leaped for the window.

B.　用動名詞片語組合下列各組句子。

　　例：Frank drank heavily.

　　　　It was his downfall.

　　　　Drinking heavily was Frank's downfall.

　　1.　We read a vivid description.

　　　　It brings us pleasure.

2. We choose words wisely.

   We, too, can create vivid pictures.

3. One must be critical of one's own work.

   It is important.

4. He trains dogs.

   It is a highly skilled profession.

C. 用不定詞片語組合下列各組句子。

例：The troops attacked the enemy.

   The general gave the order.

   The general ordered the troops *to attack the enemy*.

1. He made a bad mistake.

   He rejected his father's help.

2. He wanted to return home earlier.

   It was impossible.

3. He came.

   He wanted to tell her the news.

4. They called for help.

   We heard them.

第三節　怎樣使句子有變化

I．句子種類的變化

我們已經知道，按照構造來說，句子分為四種：簡單句、集合句、複合句和混合句。簡單句提供最直接生動的表達方式；集合句列舉項目，加以描述；複合句是表達繁複意思的最佳方式。如果有更繁複的意思要表達，還可以考慮使用混合句。不過，任何一種句子都不可過度使用。一長串的簡單句會顯得不連貫、單調而幼稚。集合句用得太多，會顯得沉悶而散漫。如果整段是複合句，在錯綜的意義限制之中會失去主要思想的線索，使讀者感到厭倦。好文章要能按照文義的需要，把這幾種句子做適當的配合。

請比較下列兩段文字：

THE SEAFOOD RESTAURANT

I was driving along the coastal highway. I saw a sign beside the road. The sign said "Seafood." I turned into the driveway. The house was freshly painted white. The smell of fresh fish greeted me. I got out of my car. A man walked out of the restaurant. I asked him what special dishes this place had to offer. He said, "Tomorrow is the grand opening." I turned away. I felt disappointed. I also

felt extremely hungry.

THE SEAFOOD RESTAURANT

As I was driving along the coastal highway, I saw a sign saying "Seafood" beside the road. I turned into the driveway and saw the new restaurant, freshly painted white. As I was getting out of my car, the smell of fresh fish greeted me. A man walked out of the restaurant. Friendly, I asked him what special dishes the place had to offer. "Tomorrow is the grand opening," he said. I turned away, feeling disappointed and extremely hungry.

第一段文字裡面所有的句子都是差不多同樣長度的簡單句。在第二段文字裡面,把複合句和簡單句交替使用,顯得更生動而有趣得多了。

就按照性質區分的句子來說,我們平常寫作所使用的大部分是敘述句,但是為了增加變化,生動有趣,可以按照內容的需要,不時穿插一些疑問句、祈使句和感嘆句。

Ⅱ. 句子成分的變化

在需要的時候,可以使用複合主詞或複合述詞。例如:

The boys and *the girls* danced all night.

The students *wrote* and *produced the play*.

The secretary *will write* or *telephone*.

Star Wars and *Superman* are movies about the good overcoming the evil.

也可以用一連串的單字、片語或子句，以求變化。例如：

Pulling, straining, pushing, lifting, we took the raft slowly downstream.

Like a couple of doctors in consultation, the two men would *point, nod, disagree, ponder*.

Whether children live *in Taipei, in Paris,* or *in Washington,* they are very much alike.

Who they are, where they live, or *what they do* seems to make little difference.

也可以使用同位語作補充說明。例如：

The rich man, *a banker*, was a criminal.

Miss Ward, *our English teacher*, was an American.

The dog, *allegedly man's best friend*, can sometimes be an awful nuisance.

His latest plan, *to organize a reading club*, sounds sensible.

The proposal *that we send a telegram to the President* was defeated.

第四節　怎樣加強句子的語氣

Ｉ．使用倒裝句

　　所謂倒裝句（inverted sentence），就是指述詞位於主詞前面的敘述句。倒裝句可以加強語氣，使句子變得更為生動有力。例如：

1. Down poured the rain.

2. Away went the car like a whirlwind.

3. Along the road roll the wagons.

4. Over the bridge marched the soldiers.

5. Ahead sat an old man.

6. Below is a restaurant.

7. In the doorway stood my mother.

8. On the very top of the hill lives a hermit.

9. Into the thick of the forest ran the wolf.

10. Across the sky rolled a strangely beautiful cloud.

11. In went the coin and out came a can of soda.

12. Slowly down the tracks steamed the train.

13. Never will I make that mistake again.

14. Nowhere have we seen the results more clearly than in Europe.

15. Not until yesterday did he change his mind.

如以上各句所示，在倒裝句中，動詞均位於主詞的前面，而且動詞的修飾詞也都放在句首。不過，這種句子的主詞若為代名詞，則主詞應

位於動詞之前，動詞的修飾詞仍置於句首。例如：

Down they flew.

Away it went.

On they marched.

Ⅱ．使用割裂句

割裂句（cleft sentence）是把一個句子重新安排，藉以強調其中的某一部分，這種句子以形式主詞 it 開始，後面接動詞 be，然後出現所要強調的部分，最後是形容詞子句。除了動詞以外，我們可以用割裂句來強調一個句子的任何部分。現以 Helen wore her best dress to the dance last night. 這個簡單句為例，我們可以把它改寫成四個割裂句，分別強調不同的部分：

It was *Helen* that(who) wore her best dress to the dance last night.

It was *her best dress* that Helen wore to the dance last night.

It was *last night* that Helen wore her best dress to the dance.

It was *to the dance* that Helen wore her best dress last night.

第一句強調主詞 Helen，第二句強調受詞 her best dress，第三句強調表示時間的副詞 last night，第四句強調表示地方的副詞片語 to the dance。除此而外，我們還可以用割裂句來強調間接受詞或受詞補語。例如：

It's *me* that she gave the picture.

It's *blue* that we've painted the living room.

怎樣寫好 英文 作文

Ⅲ． 用反詰式問句

反詰式問句（rhetorical question）是一種加強語氣的問句，它具有問句的形式，但具有敘述句的含義。例如：

Is that a reason for despair? (=Surely that is not a reason for despair.)

Can anyone doubt the wisdom of this action? (=Surely no one can doubt the wisdom of this action.)

Is no one going to defend me? (=Surely someone is going to defend me.)

Who knows? (=Nobody knows.)

What difference does it make? (=It makes no difference.)

Ⅳ． 重複主要的單字

重複一個句子裡面主要的單字，可以收到逐漸加強語氣的效果。不過，重複的次數不能太多，否則會顯得單調。所以只能偶爾用用，而且要用得恰當。例如：

He felt *more and more* angry.

He drove *more and more* slowly.

He *talked and talked and talked*.

They *knocked and knocked*.

He talked *on and on and on*.

They went *up and up*.

They hit him *again and again*.

You can find *doctors and doctors*.

There were *dogs and dogs* all over the place.

如以上例句所示，重複的字或用連接詞連接，或用逗號分開。

V．使用主動語態

一般說來，動詞的主動語態（active voice）比被動語態（passive voice）有力 。因為主動語態表示主詞是動作的做出者，而被動語態表示主詞是動作的接受者。例如：The secretary read the minutes. 就比 The minutes were read by the secretary. 有力。在下列各組句子中，後面一句為主動語態，前面一句為被動語態。

1. The cake was finished by the children.

   The children finished the cake.

2. The ball was kicked by the boy.

   The boy kicked the ball.

3. A book was bought by John the other day.

   John bought a book the other day.

4. A letter is written by Bob every day.

   Bob writes a letter every day.

5. The beach is crowded with swimmers on the weekends.

   Swimmers crowd the beach on the weekends.

6. The stereo was turned up loudly by him.

   He turned up the stereo loudly.

VI. 使用雙重否定

所謂雙重否定（double negative），就是用 not without, not uncommon 等形式來表示肯定的意思。在下列各句中，括弧內的肯定句等於前面的雙重否定句，但語氣卻不如雙重否定句來得強。

1. Not many people have nowhere to live. (=Most people have somewhere to live.)

2. She is not an unwelcome guest there. (=She is a welcome guest there.)

3. You can't do it without being caught. (=You will certainly be caught if you do it.)

4. He can't speak English without making mistakes.(=He makes mistakes when he speaks English.)

5. It is not uncommon to find it so.(=It is common to find it so.)

6. No one has nothing to offer to society.(=Everyone has something to offer to society.)

VII. 使用助動詞 do

助動詞 do 與動詞連用時可加強句子的語氣。例如：

She *does come*!

Do stop that noise!

Do be still!

Please *do be* seated.

That's exactly what Jim *did say*.

I *do want* to go with you.

Ⅷ. 使用 so+adj. or adv.+that 的句型

so+adj. or adv.+that 的句型可以用來表示加強形容詞或副詞所達到的程度。例如：

She was *so ill that* we had to send for a doctor.

He was *so angry that* he couldn't speak.

She was *so weary that* she fell.

He was *so exhausted that* he slept for 16 hours.

The statement was *so clear that* it couldn't be misunderstood.

The windows are *so small that* they don't admit much light.

The robber ran *so fast that* the policeman failed to catch him.

John worked *so hard that* he didn't go to bed until four o'clock this morning.

Ⅸ. 用 such, such that 或 such...that 的句型

such, such that 或 such...that 的句型也可以用來表示程度上的加強。例如：

I've never heard of *such* a thing!

He is *such* a liar.

We haven't had *such* fun as this in years!

The weather was *such that* we could not go out.

The force of the explosion was *such that* all the windows were

broken.

Father told us *such* a funny story *that* we all laughed.

練 習 十 八

A. 改寫下列各句，使之更為生動而有力：

1. The boxer struck his opponent quickly and surely.

2. Disorder was everywhere in the room.

3. Three Christian principles are faith, hope, and charity.

4. The soloist sang beautifully.

5. The influence of television is great.

6. The honor for the world's first newspaper goes to the Chinese;
    the credit is well deserved.

7. People everywhere all over the world want the latest news.

8. Surely life has been made richer by newspapers.

9. It seemed silly to Mother to talk about things over and done with.

10. The same old problem came at the first of every month.

B. 用下列句型各造兩個句子：

1. It was...that

2. connot...without

3. so+adj.+that

4. so+adv.+that

5. such

6. such that

7. such...that

第五章　段落

第一節　段落的形式

我們在前面已經講過，一個句子表達一個完全的意思。一段（paragraph）則表達一系列的密切關聯的意思。

每一段都是全篇文章的一部分，這個部分只就一個小主題來發揮，一段有時只有一兩句話，有時可以相當長。每段第一行的前面都有空格（通常空五個字母），這種空格叫做〔行首空格〕（indentation）,其作用在表示一個新段落的開始，也就是說，作者現在要討論一個新的主題。

一個段落常含有主題句（topic sentence），相關句（related sentence）和結尾句（concluding sentence）。主題句扼要指出全段的中心思想；相關句則提出有關的細節或例證，以支持或說明主題句所表示的中心思想；結尾句則就整段的討論作一簡單的結論。

假定作文的題目是 Steam，我們要在這一段裡討論 steam 的各種用途。那麼，最好以第一句為主題句，把主要的意思表達出來。

第一句　One of the greatest advantages of steam power is its applicability
　　　　to a wide range of activities.

我們已經在這個句子裡指出 steam 的用途，但是意思很空泛，必須說得更明確些。在進一步發揮或詳細說明（amplify）時，我們可以在第二句裡指出 steam 的用途同人類日常生活的關係。

第二句　When James Watt saw steam lifting the lid of the kettle, it is probable that even he did not realize in how many ways steam would exert an influence on the life of man.

　　我們已經指出 steam 可以應用在人類生活的許多方面，現在必須把這個論點加以證明。我們可以在第三、四、五、六句裡舉出交通、工業和動力作為例證。

第三句　Steam has, indeed, brought about vast changes; its application to transport has enabled us to make journeys by rail at what our ancestors would have regarded as fantastic speeds, and to make journeys by sea in five days which took them nearly three months.

第四句　In industry, steam has replaced the water mill and the treadmill, and, in the earliest days of the Industrial Revolution, the machinery in coal mines, cotton or wool factories was driven directly by steam.

第五句　Now that steam is used to genetrate electricity in gigantic power stations, its adaptability is greatly increased, for everyone knows how versatile and how vital electrical power is.

第六句　Not even nuclear energy can beat steam for producing clean, safe power.

　　關於 steam 的用途，我們已經舉出四個例子，現在可以總結（sum up）一下。

第七句　These are only three instances out of many which demonstrate how steam can be applied to a very wide range of activities indeed.

現在我們可以把這七個句子連在一起，成為完整的一段：

One of the greatest advantages of steam power is its applicability to a wide range of activities. When James Watt saw steam lifting the lid of his kettle, it is probable that even he did not realize in how many ways steam would exert an influence on the life of man. Steam has, indeed, brought about vast changes; its application to transport has enabled us to make journeys by rail at what our ancestors would have regarded as fantastic speeds, and to make journeys by sea in five days which took them nearly three months. In industry, steam has replaced the water mill and the treadmill, and, in the earliest days of the Industrial Revolution, the machinery in coal mines, cotton or wool factories was driven directly by steam. Now that steam is used to generate electricity in gigantic power stations, its adaptability is greatly increased, for everyone knows how versatile and how vital electrical power is. Not even nuclear energy can beat steam for producing

clean, safe power. These are only three instances out
of many which demonstrate how steam can be
applied to a very wide range of activities indeed.

　　在寫上面這段作文時，我們最關切的是如何把資料按照適當的順序加以安排。關於 steam 的用途，我們所採取的排列方式是先作一個一般性的說明，然後舉出三個細節來支持那個說明。

　　在寫作的過程中，意思的連貫也不能忽視。先從一般性的說明開始，進而提出一些特殊的例證，這種方法有助於整個意思的連貫。但是，表達那些意思的字句也應該構成一個連貫的順序，也就是說，各個句子措辭要彼此關聯，前後呼應。

第二節　主題句

正如我們在第一節中說的,每一段文字常有一個主題句(topic sentence),扼要指出全段的中心思想。主題句通常出現在一段文字的開頭,但有時也會出現在一段的中間或末尾,也可以沒有主題句,而實際上全段文字仍然集中於一個中心思想,成為一段結構良好的文章,尤以敘述文為然。現在請仔細閱讀下面三段不同的文字,並注意各段主題句(以斜體字印刷者)的位置:

1. 下面是 Christopher Morley的 "On Making Friends" 中的一段;作者以愛默生所說的話為主題句,並且把它放在這一段文字的開頭:

   Emerson is right in saying that friendship can't be hurried. It takes time to ripen. It needs a background of humorous, wearisome, or even tragic events shared together, a certain tract of memories shared in common, so that you know your own life and your companion's have really moved for some time in the same channel. It needs interchange of books, meals together, discussion of one another's whims with mutual friends, to gain a proper perspective. It is set in a rich haze of half—remembered occasions, sudden glimpses, ludicrous pranks, unsuspected observations, midnight confidences when heart spoke to candid heart.

2. 下面是一篇以 "My Kid Sister" 為題的作文中的一段；全段的主題句出現在這一段文字的中央：

> She is good. She is good to her family, better to her friends, and best to herself. She is shrewd. She is shrewd with her teachers, shrewder with her friends, and shrewdest with me. *Oh, she has many admirable characteristics*. She is bright and alert. She is bright and alert with younger children, she is brighter and more alert with guests, and she is brightest and most alert with boys. Yes, she is like a human violin, responding sensitively to the touch of circumstance.

3. 下面是描寫 Frank 的一段文字；從這一段的開頭到接近末尾的部分，作者提出有力的證據，以證明出現在末尾的主題句所表示的中心思想：

> When Frank first slithered up beside me in the library and asked to see my sociology homework, I didn't think much about it. Later I discovered that he submitted a copy of my book review for his own homework. Still, I wanted to trust him. I was not even suspicious when he moved to sit across the aisle from me in our math class. It was Mr. Brown, our teacher, who detected his wandering eyes that time. Two weeks later I noticed that Frank wasn't

doing any of the activities required in chemistry lab. Instead, he was wandering around the room making mental notes of the results other students were getting so he could write his report. Although I like to think positively about others, I had to face the hard fact. *Frank was a cheat!*

練 習 十 九

A. 指出下面三段文字中的主題句，並在下面畫一底線表示之：

1. An air of calmness filled the valley. Enclosing the valley with wide green arms, the mountains seemed to protect it securely from the outside world. Two or three farmhouses slept in the sun. A cow or two under the trees of the pasture ate contentedly. The tiny white church surrounded by its little graveyard accentuated the quiet of the scene. Truly, it seemed a place in which one might find peace.

2. The accident rate that winter was frightening. Three of our lumbermen were struck by falling trees, eight were cut by saws, and two had their hands cut off by tractor treads. As many as fifteen lumbermen were gashed by axes each month. The insurance report at the end of the season showed a total of 102

injuries, all of them, fortunately, nonfatal.

3. The older I grow, the more I appreciate children. Now, on my 80th birthday, I salute them again. Children are the most wholesome part of the human race, the sweetest, for they are freshest form the hand of God. Playful, creative, mischievous, they fill the world with joy and good humor. We adults live a life of worry as to what they will think of us; a life of defense against their terrifying energy; a life of hard work to live up to their great expectations. We put them to bed with a sense of relief—and greet them in the morning with delight and anticipation. We envy them the freshness of adventure and the discovery of life. In all these ways, children add to the wonder of being alive. In all these ways, they help to keep us young.

B.　用下列主題句各寫一段文章：

1. Teamwork is essential in basketball.

2. I often learn new English words by listening to the radio.

3. Working hard is the key to success.

4. Using a dictionary is helpful.

5. Swimming is great fun in summer.

6. It is wrong to cheat in an examination.

第三節 段落的統一性

所謂段落的統一性（unity），就是指一段文字當中所有的細節，都應該與主題句所包含的中心思想或本段的主題有密切關係。今以下面一段美國學生的習作為例，詳加分析，以說明的段落的統一性。（為便於討論起見，在各句前面加有號碼。）

GETTYSBURG, A HISTORIC AMERICAN SHRINE

(1) Gettysburg is a historic shrine. (2) There is a battlefield of twenty-five square miles. (3) Many people drive along the beautiful roads on the field. (4) Picnic parties come in great numbers on holidays to see the monuments erected by the various states. (5) Guides are everywhere. (6) They take tourists over the field and explain the battle. (7) There is a cyclorama in which is a large painting of the battle. (8) The headquarters of Lee and Meade are still preserved. (9) Many known and unknown soldiers are buried in the national Cemetery. (10) Lincoln spoke here. (11) He gave his immortal "Gettysburg Address." (12) Several Presidents of the United States have delivered talks here on Memorial Day. (13) The town was here during the battle. (14) It

1893 Congress designated it as a national park.

　　上面這段作文是描寫美國歷史上有名的聖地蓋提茲堡（Pennsylvania 州一城鎮，為南北戰爭的戰場，並有安葬該次戰役陣亡將士的國家公墓）。一個學生在寫這段作文之前要是對 shrine 這個字沒有清楚的認識，就應該設法明白該字的含義。他要是對所要討論的中心思想沒有透徹的了解，那他寫出來的東西就會不知所云，因而破壞整段文字的統一性。

　　在上面這段作文中，第一句是主題句，指出全段的中心思想，本句中最重要的字是 shrine。第二句指出該地是個 battlefield 的事實，以支持前面的主題句。第三句指出，有很多人駕車駛過那些漂亮的道路；不知道此一事實與 Gettysburg 之成為 shrine 有何關聯?不能因為該地遊客如織就稱之為 shrine。第四句中的兩個細節也和主題句沒有多大關係；因為 Picnic parties 並不是使該地成為 shrine的因素，那些 monuments 也是在戰爭結束很久以後才建立的。第五、六兩句敘述 guides，這也和 Gettysburg 成為 shrine 扯不上關係。第七句中描繪南北戰爭的圓形畫景可能使畫家和遊客感到興趣，但對主題句的中心思想毫無助益。

　　第八句指出 Lee 和 Meade 的司令部，此乃戰爭期間重要決策的所在地，有助於 Gettysburg 之成為 shrine。第九句所指出的陣亡將士墓，更闡明了主題句的中心思想。第十、十一兩句中，林肯和他的著名演講也是使得 Gettysburg 成為 shrine 的因素。第十二句不應該列入這一段，因為後來的美國總統是在 Gettysburg 已經成為 shrine 之後才

　　上面這段作文是描寫

在此地演講的。第十三句應該保留，因為該鎮實為戰場的一部分。第十四句提到目前的人口，這跟本段的中心思想無關，應該刪掉。第十五句指出美國國會把 Gettysburg 定為國家公園，只不過是對該地業已成為 shrine 的事實加以肯定罷了，所以這個句子也不是十分必要的。

　　前面那段作文經過仔細分析之後，十五個句子當中就有七個句子與主題句的中心思想無關，應該刪掉。下面這段文字便是經過刪節以後的面貌，雖然比原來那段短了很多，但剩下的各項事實均能切合主題，使全段作文更具有統一性：

　　　　Gettysburg is a historic shrine. There is a battlefield of twenty-five square miles. The headquarters of Lee and Meade are still preserved. Many known and unknown soldiers are buried in the National Cemetery. Lincoln spoke here. He gave his immortal " Gettysburg Address." The town was here during the battle. In 1893 Congress designated it as a national park.

第四節　段落的連貫性

　　一段文章的細節不但要與主題句或中心思想有密切的關係,而且要按照一定的順序排列,才能使整段文章上下啣接,前後呼應,具有連貫性(coherence)。一段文章的細節通常按照下面三種順序排列:時間的順序(chronological order)、空間順序(spatial order)和邏輯的順序(logical order)。

Ⅰ. 時間的順序

　　所謂時間的順序(chronological order),就是要把一段文章中的各個細節,按照時間的先後或是事情發生的先後來排列;這種方法可以用來敘述一連串的歷史事件,也可以用來介紹某一過程的各個步驟。下面是一位美國學生 Tom Kelly 所寫的作文當中的一段,他把自己看做汽車的發明人,描寫試車成功的經過:

> I saw his hand drop. My foot touched the
> accelerator. The machine began to vibrate and the
> last mechanic jumped aside. With a tremendous
> shudder, we moved forward, slowly at first, but
> faster and faster and faster. I glanced at the
> speedometer, blinked, and had to look again. It was
> incredible, impossible, but after a quick check of the
> instruments I knew that the speedometer was right. I
> was sure that my machine was a success. I had

proven that man could go as fast as he had dreamed. I was traveling at 20 miles an hour. The automobile was now a reality, and I was the first to drive it.

II. 空間的順序

空間的順序（spatial order）多用於寫景，也就是說，在寫景時一定要按照從左到右或從右到左，由前到後或由後到前的順序；切不可忽左忽右或忽前忽後，使讀者摸不著頭腦。現在請看 James Hiser 如何在 "Filipino Barber Shop" 一文的一段中描寫一家理髮店：

> I seated myself in the barber chair, which was only an old, straight-backed object made of bamboo placed on a wooden box in the center of the room. Directly in front of this throne hung a dull, blurred mirror, suspended by ropes from the roof. To my right stood a square table, upon which rested the barber's only tools—a pair of clippers, a dirty-looking comb, and a razor. As I looked downward, I was somewhat surprised to find that the floor was still in its natural state—dirt. It also showed evidence that hair had been cut here before. I noticed now for the first time an opening at the rear, over which a piece of gray material hung. Evidently this passageway led into the living quarters of the barber.

III. 邏輯的順序

所謂邏輯的順序（logical order），就是要把具有相互關係的概念作合理的安排，使讀者能由前一概念了解後一概念，進而了解整段文章的大意。現在請看紐約時報如何在一篇社論 "The Ultimatum" 的一段中將有關的概念作合理的安排：

The Allied terms were as fair and as generous as they could afford to be, considering Japan's long record of aggression. The Japanese people were told that we have no intention to enslave them as a nation or destroy them as a race. They were told that we have no designs of their home islands. They were told that we wish them to enjoy a government in which fundamental human rights will be respected. They were told that after the war they will be permitted to maintain such industries as will sustain their economy and permit the exaction of just reparations. They were told that to this end they will be given access to, though not control of, raw materials. And they were told that they could expect eventual participation in world trade relations.

練 習 二 十

　　在下列 A、B、C 三個練習中，各句在原作中的順序已被攪亂並加以編號；請找出各句正確的順序，並在各號碼前面的空白內寫上 a、b 或 c 等表示之（a 表示第一句，b 表示第二句，c 表示第三句，其餘的由此類推）。

例： _c_　1.　She answered it with a curt "Hello"

　　 _e_　2.　It was Rhonda.

　　 _a_　3.　It was on the evening of her second week at home.

　　 _d_　4.　The sound of the voice that greeted her seemed to reach out with almost physical power, tearing through her.

　　 _b_　5.　The phone rang.

A.　____　1.　She was very understanding, but it didn't happen again.

　　____　2.　I brought them here with me and shall keep them in my heart forever.

　　____　3.　The first section stayed in the same room, the second went to another.

　　____　4.　No, I will never forget those warm and wonderful memories.

_____ 5. All of us, in a delightful mood, stood giggling and choking with laughter as our teacher searched for us up and down the stairways!

_____ 6. I remember that, on one April Fool's Day, fifteen girls hid in a corner of the hall instead of reporting to our room.

B. _____ 1. I look in the mirror and see the beginnings of a beard.

_____ 2. Man makes elaborate plans for the future because he realizes that all too soon it will be the present.

_____ 3. Being drawn back into reality, I think of the future.

_____ 4. When I look back on the past seventeen years of my life, it seems like one day with many events crowded into it.

_____ 5. I plan for the day when it will be the present.

_____ 6. Only a minute ago I was learning long division; I thought high school was a hallowed place never to be attained.

C. _____ 1. No one knew what could be expected from it; but it was my own idea and my own invention, and I had to test it.

_____ 2. A warm beam of light had fallen upon my face.

_____ 3. My mind was about to collapse under the intense strain.

_____ 4. It was a bright sunny day when I awoke.

_____ 5. This morning might be my last; this was the thought that constantly went through my mind, for today was the day that I was to test the new machine.

第五節　承轉詞

承轉詞（transitional expressions）是指用來表示前後各句的含義具有相互關係的字或片語。承轉詞乃是各句之間的「橋樑」。在一段文章中，除了統一性和連貫性以外，我們還得用適當的承轉詞，才能使整段文章絲絲入扣，一氣呵成。現在請閱讀下面一段文字：

> I was accepted and started work. My experience had been derived chiefly from books. I was not prepared for the difficult period of adjustment. I soon became discouraged with myself and so dissatisfied with my job that I was on the point of quitting. My employer must have sensed this. He called me into his office and talk to me about the duties of my position and the opportunities for advancement. I realized that there was nothing wrong with me or the job and I decided to stay.

一般說來，這段文字相當不錯，很有統一性，細節的安排也很有條理，可惜讀起來有些生硬，不夠流暢。現在請看看同一段經過稍微修改以後的面貌：

> I was accepted, and started work. *Until that time* my experience had been derived chiefly from books, *and unfortunately* those books had not prepared me for the difficult period of adjustment

that every inexperienced secretary must face in a new position. Consequently I soon became *so* discouraged with myself and so dissatisfied with the job *that* I was on the point of quitting. *I think* My employer must have sensed this, *for* he called me into his office and talked to me about *both* the duties of my position and the opportunities *it offered* for advancement. *That talk helped me considerably. From then on,* I realized that there was nothing wrong with me or the job *that experience could not cure,* and I decided to stay.

上面兩段文字內容完全一樣，用字也沒有很大的差異，但是第二段文字顯然比第一段文字好得多，讀起來比較通順。這是因為作者在第二段文字中增添了承轉詞及別的字句，使得各句的意思更具有連貫性。

常用的承轉詞可分為下面九種：

1. 表示時間的承轉詞

after a short (long) time	lately	since
after a while	presently	then
afterward	recently	temporarily
at last	since then	thereafter

2. 表示再者或此外的承轉詞：

again	besides	in addition
also	further	likewise
and	furthermore	moreover
and then		

3. 表示對比或反對的承轉詞

after all	in spite of	on the other hand
but	nevertheless	it must be confessed
despite	notwithstanding	still
however	on the contrary	yet
in contrast		

4. 表示比較或相似的承轉詞：

in a like manner	in the same way
likewise	similarly

5. 表示讓步或接受事實的承轉詞：

after all	at the same time	of course
although	granted	perhaps
and yet	naturally	

6. 表示順序的承轉詞：

first	in the first place	then
second	in the second place	finally
third	next	last

7. 表示例證的承轉詞：

for example	in fact	particularly
for instance	in other words	specifically
incidentally	in particular	that is
indeed	namely	

8. 表示結果的承轉詞：

accordingly	then	as a result
consequently	therefore	thereby
hence	thus	

9. 表示總結的承轉詞：

in brief	in short	to conclude
in conclusion	on the whole	to summarize

練 習 二 十 一

A. 仔細閱讀下面一段文字，找出其中的承轉詞並畫底線表示之：

Some people remember the things they are supposed to do by writing notes to themselves. Then they leave the notes in obvious places, such as on the kitchen counter or on the floor in the middle of the living room. I've never been convinced that writing notes to myself does much good. Most of the time I lose them or forget to look at them until it's

too late. I prefer to use an alarm clock to remind myself of things I'm supposed to do. I have ten alarm clocks in my house which I use to remind myself about things. For example, if I have to make a telephone call at a certain time, I'll set an alarm clock to go off a few minutes early and put the clock by the telephone. Or if I want to watch a certain television program, I'll set an alarm clock at the right time and put the clock on top of the TV set. I can remember almost anything I want to if I use my clocks. There is, however, one drawback to my system. Sometimes an alarm goes off and I don't know what it means. I always remember setting it, but not why I set it. If the clock is by the telephone, I know I may have set it to remind me to call someone, but I can't be sure. I might have set it to remind myself that somebody was to call me at a certain time.

B. 仔細閱讀下面三段文字，並根據上下文將下列承轉詞分別填入各空白內：

| also | but | for example | furthermore |
| however | indeed | therefore | yet |

Curiosity is a good, positive reason for deciding to travel. Friends take trips and tell interesting stories about the people and places. _____ , curious people want to learn by traveling, learning through their own experience. They buy tickets and go off to new places where they find unusual situations and adventure. They _____ find out some things about themselves.

_____ , there are some people who travel with another reason in mind. These people are traveling away from real troubles toward imagined solutions. People with problems at home sometimes travel to get away from such problems. Emerson's words are important to these people. Emerson meant that on a trip a traveler might be looking for a better situation or for an improvement. ____ , Emerson believed, the person will find only the happiness that he or she brought along. There are no new supplies in new places.

There are many inferences that can be made from Emerson's words. _____ , a good student at home will be a good student abroad. A person who likes other people and was well-liked at home will

find friends all over the world. _____ , a troubled person will not find true answers—only temporary distractions. Travel will provide other things to think about, _____ the real problems do not disappear. Travel can _____ help a person to broaden horizons; travel can satisfy curiosity and make a person more aware of problems and possible solutions.

第六章　標點符號

　　英文裡常用的標點符號（punctuation marks）計有：句號（.），逗號（,），分號（；），冒號（：），問號（?），驚嘆號（!），引號（"…"或'…'）撇號（'），破折號（—），省略號（...），圓括號（　），方括號〔　〕，連字號（-）。標點符號的目的在使讀者有清楚的概念。使用標點符號時一定要有充分的理由，切不可濫用，特別是逗號。茲將各種標點符號的用法分述如下：

Ⅰ．句號（.）

1.　句號（period）主要是用在敘述句的末尾，但在現代用法中，有時也用在祈使句和驚嘆句的末尾。

> Today is Tuesday.
>
> We have three days to go.
>
> Be careful of the step.
>
> Let's forget the whole matter.
>
> How pleasant it would be to be there now.

2.　句號可用在各種縮寫字的後面。

　　(1)　稱號：Col., Dr., Hon., Mrs., Rev.

　　(2)　學位：B.A., B.S., M.D., Ph.D.

　　(3)　名字：John A. Jones; Robert W. Brown

(4) 月份：Jan., Feb., Aug., Nov.

(5) 美國州名：Ala., Ga., Me., I11., Wash.

(6) 其他：Ave., St., vol., p., etc., U.S.A., B.C., A.D.

3. 句號可用在小數的前面以及圓和分之間。

The error is less than .01 inch.

The correct answer is 57.39.

The price tag read $11.98.

Ⅱ. 逗號（,）

1. 逗號（comma）可用來連接由 and, but, or, for, nor 和 so 所連接的兩個子句，但兩個子句很短時，則可不用逗號。

He took the medicine, and his cold got better.

He lost his keys, and his wife was angry.

I would like to accept your invitation, but I will be out of town on that date.

There was nothing more that we could do, so we went home.

2. 逗號可用在一連串的單字、片語或子句之間。

He promised them only blood, sweat, toil, and tears.

Reading, swimming, and dancing are my favorite recreations.

It was said of Washington that he was first in war, first in peace, and first in the hearts of his countrymen.

We were tired, hungry, and cold.

The professor gave a long, dull, but exceedingly learned lecture.

We looked in the house, in the garden, and in the barn, but we could not find the cat.

3. 逗號可用在位於句首的片語或副詞子句之後，使之與主要子句分開。

   When we finally got home after our long trip, we felt as though we had never been away.

   Unused to so much excitement, the child fell asleep.

   Pulling over to the side of the road at the first opportunity, I waited for the fire engines to pass.

   If there is going to be any difficulty about this request, I would rather withdraw it.

   Being ignorant of the facts of the situation, I could say nothing.

   If I go, you'll be sorry.

4. 逗號可用在插入語和非限制性形容詞子句的前後。

   Soldiers, who are selected by physical fitness tests, should show a lower sickness rate than that of the total population.

   This book, which I hope you will read soon, gives a complete account of that important event.

   The soldiers, weary and footsore, straggled up the road.

This is, I believe, the first time such a thing has ever happened here.

5. 逗號可用於下列各項：

(1) 日期。

October 10, 1983

January 1, 1984

(2) 地址。

No .5, Alley 2, Lane 70, Hsin Sheng S. Road, Sec. 3, Taipei,

Taiwan, Republic of China

(3) 數字。

22,745; 1,000,000; 150,743,290

(4) 稱號。

R. W. Leeds, M.D.

John Cook, Captain of the Guard

(5) 直接稱呼。

Look, John!

Yes, Mary, it is.

I would like to ask you, Mr. Jones, for your opinion.

I think, madam, that you had better leave.

Sir, I'd like to ask a question.

(6) 正式信函的稱呼。

Dear Mother,

Dear Joe,

Dear Mr. Wang,

(7) 信函結尾表示敬意的套語。

Sincerely yours,

Yours very truly,

(8) 直接引語及主要子句之間。

He said, "You are only half right."

"This," I said, "is the last straw."

"Nobody asked you, sir," she said.

"But," he asked, "what if they refuse? "

William said, "Come here."

"I don't know," Lee said, " of a better place."

(9) 連接副詞　however, moreover, therefore, consequently 等的前後（或後面）。

Jim likes Pete; however, I don't care for him.

We thought, moreover, that we could get away with it.

There was a chance, on the other hand, that prices would go up.

You must try, first of all, to consider it objectively.

Ⅲ.　分號（；）

1.　分號（semicolon）可用來連接兩個有密切關聯的獨立子句。

Try this one; it seems to be your color.

His mother won't let him go; she is afraid he might get hurt.

Your car is new; mine is eight years old.

Take care of the children; the adults can take care of themselves.

It was not the hours or the wages that discouraged me; it was the constant monotony of the work.

2. 分號可用在兩個獨立子句之間的連接副詞之前。

It won't work; therefore there is no sense in buying it.

His argument has some merit; however, he goes too far.

His eyes went bad; consequently, he had to resign his position as a proofreader.

3. 分號可用來分隔一系列含有逗號的片語。

For officers we elected Jim Brown, the banker, as president; Cliff Burns, superintendent of schools, as vice president; Mark Harmon, the well-known lawyer, as secretary; and Steve Granger, an officer of the textile company, as treasurer.

Ⅳ． 冒號（：）

1. 冒號（colon）可用在兩個子句之間，以表示後面那個子句旨在說明、重述或闡述前面一個子句。

They raised the tuition for one reason only: they could not operate on the current revenue.

2. 冒號可用在一個句子的後面，以表示下面還有細目或說明。

There are three ways to get there: by car, by bus, or by plane.

3. 冒號可用在較長的引用句之前。

This is his statement as reported in the papers: " I have never

advocated such ideas; I do not advocate them now; I do not approve of them; and I have no reason for believing that I ever will approve of them."

4. 冒號還可以用於下列各項：

   (1)   正式信函的稱呼之後。

       Dear Mr. Jackson:

   (2)   小時與分的數字之間。

       12：00   2：45

Ⅴ．問號（？）

1. 問號（question mark）多半是用在問句之後，一個問句即使看起來像敘述句，後面照樣可以用問號。

   How did he do it?

   He did?

   Whose is this?

   You mean he's ill?

2. 問號有時可用在括弧中，表示對前面一個字的正確性有疑問。

   These amateurs (?) make a comfortable living out of sports.

   His funny (?) remarks were more than I could bear.

   注意：間接問句或由疑問詞所引導的子句後面不要用問號。

   He asked me how I did it.

   I wonder why she said that.

VI． 驚嘆號（！）

驚嘆號（exclamation mark）可用在祈使句或感嘆句之後。

> Be quiet!
>
> Attention!
>
> Leave the room at once!
>
> Oh, you fool!
>
> God help us!
>
> How wonderful!

VII． 引號（"…" 或 '…'）

引號（quotation marks）分為雙引號（double quotation marks）和單引號（single quotation marks），通常成對使用。

1. 雙引號可用在直接引語的前後。

> I said, "That's your worry."
>
> "Bob," he said, "you can't do that!"
>
> "What is the matter? " she asked.
>
> He said, " I believe this is a good solution to the problem."

2. 雙引號可用在取自某作家的比較短的引用文中。

> Esther, on the contrary, is always trying hard "to be industrious, contented, and true-hearted, and to do some good to some one, and win some love."

3. 雙引號可用在句子裡面，以表示畫、短的音樂作品、短詩、書的章節、船等的名稱。

Leonardo da Vinci's "Mona Lisa"

Tchaikovsky's "Swan Lake"

Emerson's "On Friendship"

4. 雙引號可用在所要討論的字的前後。

"Warbling" is a musical word.

The word "garage" comes from the French; the word " piano" comes from the Italian.

5. 雙引號可用來指出某人所用的詞句，作者對該詞句可能有異議。

His " mechanical invention," like most of his other bright ideas, didn't work.

6. 單引號用於引用語中的引用語。

The boy replied, "My father always told me, 'John, don't do anything hastily.'"

VIII. 撇號（'）

1. 撇號（apostrophe）可用以表示字母的省略。

I've, can't, hasn't, didn't, o'clock, it's（it is）

2. 撇號可用在字母或數字的複數形式中。

Let's begin with the A's; look under the K's; the S's look like 8's.

3. 撇號可用來表示名詞或代名詞的所有格。

boy's, girl's, ox's, mouse's, tooth's, antenna's

men's, women's, oxen's, mice's, teeth's, antennae's

anybody's, anyone's, everybody's, one's, nobody's, someone's

James's, Charles's, Keats's, Burns's, Dickens's

注意：James's, Charles's 等也可以寫成 James', Charles'等。

IX. 破折號（一）

1. 破折號（dash）可用來強調句子末尾的一個字或片語。

   In the whole world there is only one person he really admires—himself.

   There is only one way to describe it—terrible!

   Absence makes the heart grow fonder—of somebody else.

2. 破折號可用來總結或結束一個複雜的句子。

   To live as free men in a free country; to enjoy, even to abuse, the right to think and speak as we like; to feel that the state is the servant of its people; to be, even in a literal sense, a trustee and a partner in the conduct of a nation—all this is what democracy means to us.

3. 破折號可用來表示引用語的中斷或未完。

   "I'd like to," he said, "but I'm—"

   "You're what?" I asked.

   "Well, I'm—I—you see, I've never done anything like that before."

4. 破折號可用在插入語的前後。

   There will never again be—you may be sure of this—so glorious an opportunity.

   This answer—if we can call it an answer—is completely meaningless.

X. 省略號（...）

省略號（ellipsis）可用來表示引用文中一個字或若干字的省略。省略的部分在句子中間時，用三個句點表示之；省略的部分在句子末尾時，則用四個句點表示之。

Death is at all times solemn, but never so much as at sea. A man dies on shore, his body remains with his friends, ...but when a man falls overboard at sea and is lost, there is a sadness in the event, and a difficulty in realizing it....

XI. 圓括號（ ）

1. 圓括號（parentheses）可用來括入說明或例子。

His wife (he married about a year ago) is a member of a very fine New England family.

Foreign words (*data*, for example) slowly become naturalized and lose their foreign characteristics.

2. 圓括號可用來括入參看的資料。

(See Appendix A), (See page 271), (Consult *Webster's Biographical Dictionary*).

3. 在正式商業信函中，圓括號可用來重述前面提到的金額。

I enclose three hundred dollars ($ 300.00) to cover my share of the costs.

XII. 方括號〔 〕

方括號（brackets）主要用來括入編者的說明或意見，換句話說，方括號裡的文字是原作裡面沒有的，而是編者自己加進去的。

He〔the American Indian〕has left his stamp upon America.

I have written to〔name of correspondent illegible〕that I will not get involved in the matter.

XIII. 連字號 (一)

1. 連字號（hyphen）可用來表示轉行時行尾的斷字。

   From Baltimore we traveled by train to Washington. 注意：

   (1) 轉行時單音節的字不能斷字。

      brought, desk, life, which, worn.

   (2) 轉行斷字時一行的末尾及下一行的開頭都不能有單是一個字母的音節。

   (3) 分音節沒有把握時最好查查字典。

2. 連字號可用來連接複合字（compound word）。

   mother-in-law, self-interest, self-reliance.

3. 連字號可用來連接表示二十一到九十九之間的數目的複合字。

   thirty-three, fifty-five, seventy-nine

4. 連字號可用來連接出現在名詞前面的複合形容詞

   The sleek, high-stepping horses paraded around the track.

   The horses parading around the track were sleek and high stepping.

在字尾為 ly 的副詞及它所修飾的形容詞之間不用連字號。

Mother gave George a gently worded rebuke.

練 習 二 十 二

抄寫下列各句，並用紅筆加上適當的標點符號；如有任何句子不需要另加標點符號，則該句可不抄。

1. He said I propose to transfer at the end of the semester.

2. Dr J A Frazer was born on March 18 1901.

3. Dr Koch a German scientist discovered the tuberculosis bacillus.

4. The lecturer was the Rev Nelson Laird D D

5. Have you read his latest book

6. The manuscript was dirty blotched and unevenly typed.

7. I have not seen him since his wife left he has been keeping to himself.

8. Mr. Reynolds the insurance man called.

9. She is quite inexperienced and has never worked in an office before.

10. See the new revolutionary car of the year the Ford.

11. She said, When I asked his opinion, he answered, I don't give advice on such questions.

12. I am enclosing eighty-five dollars $85.00 for the semiannual premium.

13. He looked at it enviously. It's a beauty he exclaimed.

14. However I still have five payments to make.

15. That she won't like it may be taken for granted.

16. Do you think he will accept she asked

17. Ladies and gentlemen it is a privilege to speak to you.

18. Aftre they took off from the airport we felt very sad.

19. Of course she explained he will be here only a few days.

20. The singular form is mouse the plural form is mice.

21. A day's work well done is a stepping stone to the success of the following day's work.

22. Jim presented a well planned program at the club meeting yesterday.

23. There were twenty two members in attendance.

24. The Johnsons take pride in their neatly trimmed lawn.

25. There is much give and take in our classroom discussions.

總　練　習

就下列各題目及其提示各寫一段八十字左右的作文。

1.　題目：My Father

　　提示：1)　How old is your father?

　　　　　2)　What does he look like?

　　　　　3)　What is his educational background?

　　　　　4)　What is his occupation?

　　　　　5)　What are his likes and dislikes?

　　　　　6)　How does he treat his children?

　　　　　7)　What do you think of him?

2.　題目：My Mother

　　提示：1)　How old is your mother?

　　　　　2)　What does she look like?

　　　　　3)　What is her educational background?

　　　　　4)　What is her occupation?

　　　　　5)　What are her likes and dislikes?

　　　　　6)　How does she treat her children?

　　　　　7)　What do you think of her?

3.　題目：One of My High School Teachers

　　提示：1)　What is his or her name?

　　　　　2)　What does he or she look like?

　　　　　3)　What subject (s) did he or she teach you?

　　　　　4)　How did he (or she) treat his or her students?

　　　　　5)　What do you think of him or her?

4.　題目：A Friend of Mine

　　提示：1)　What is his or her name?

　　　　　2)　When and how did you become friends?

　　　　　3)　What are his or her likes and dislikes?

　　　　　4)　What do you usually do together?

　　　　　5)　What do you think of your friend?

5.　題目：An Unforgettable Person

　　提示：1)　What is the name of the person?

　　　　　2)　What does he or she look like?

　　　　　3)　What makes him or her unforgettable?

　　　　　4)　What do you think of him or her?

6.　題目：An Unforgettable Day

　　提示：1)　What was the day?

　　　　　2)　Where were you on that day?

3) What did you do on that day?

4) What made that day unforgettable?

7. 題目：A Trip

提示：
1) On what day did you take the trip?

2) Where did you go?

3) With whom did you go?

4) How did you get there?

5) How long did you stay there?

6) What did you do there?

7) When did you leave for home?

8) What do you think of the trip?

8. 題目：A Scenic Spot

提示：
1) Where is the spot?

2) How can you get there?

3) What is the scenery like there?

4) What can you do there?

5) What do you think of the spot?

9. 題目：A Shopping Experience

提示：
1) On what day did you have this experience?

2) Where did you go shopping?

3) With whom did you go shopping?

4) What were you going to buy?

5) How much did you spend?

6) Why do you remember this experience?

10. 題目：My Favorite Pastime

提示：1) What is your favorite pastime?

2) When did you take it up?

3) How often do you enjoy doing it?

4) Why do you like it more than some other pastime?

5) What have you learned from it?

11. 題目：My Favorite Movie

提示：1) What is the name of the movie?

2) When and where did you see it?

3) With whom did you see it?

4) What is the movie chiefly about?

5) Why is it you favorite movie?

12. 題目：The Book That Influenced Me Most

提示：1) What is the title of the book?

2) Who is the author?

3) When did you read it?

4)　How long did it take you to finish it?

5)　What is the book chiefly about?

6)　How did the book influence you more than some other book?

13. 題目：The Person I Admire Most

提示：1)　Who is the person you admire most?

2)　How did you come to know him or her?

3)　What kind of person is he or she?

4)　What does he or she usually do?

5)　Why do you admire him or her most?

14. 題目：The Importance of Education

提示：1)　Why is education important?

2)　How important is education to an individual?

3)　How important is education to society?

4)　How important is education to the country?

5)　What is the best way to promote education in general?

15. 題目：The Importance of Exercise

提示：1)　Why is exercise important?

2)　Who should exercise?

3)　How often should one exercise?

4) When should one exercise?

5) What exercise is good for you? Why?

16. 題目：The Importance of Science

提示：1) Why is science important?

2) What benefits has science brought to mankind?

17. 題目：On Friendship

提示：1) Why is friendship important?

2) What kind of people do you like to make friends with?

3) What is the best way to make friends with other people?

4) What is the best way to establish a lasting friendship?

18. 題目：On Honesty

提示：1) Why should one be honest?

2) What might happen if one is not honest?

19. 題目：On Love

提示：1) What is love?

2) Why is love important?

習題解答

練 習 一

主　詞	述　詞
1. The boy	Worked very hard.
2. She	helped her mother after school.
3. His father	ran a small barbershop.
4. A box of pencils	is lying on the desk.
5. A salesman	knocked at the door one afternoon.
6. She	is an unusually talented pianist.
7. A boy with a fine mind	should continue his education.
8. The two women	looked at each other sadly.
9. He	should take a full-time job now.
10. The little girl in the cottage	looked out from the window.
11. His friends	came to his aid.
12. They	raised ten thousand dollars for him.
13. The old woman	lay in bed quietly.
14. Most of the leaves	have fallen.
15. They	were married before long.
16. Their friendship	was based on mutual honesty and trust.
17. The energetic young man	achieved one success after another.
18. People	breathlessly waited for the outcome of the race.
19. Cheering crowds of people	lined the streets.
20. He	was, indeed, a very famous man.

練 習 二

B. 1. Have men been swimming for a long time?

2. Do people swim for fun and exercise?

3. Do most cities have public pools?

4. Are some people afraid of learning to swim?

5. Is it true that bodies float naturally?

6. Can most people learn to swim if they try?

7. Can babies less than one year old learn to swim?

8. Can some babies learn to swim before they learn to walk?

9. Can swimming slow down signs of aging?

10. Is swimming good for the heart and lungs?

11. Has swimming helped many people look young and healthy?

12. Should people be careful when swimming and diving?

13. Is swimming in a place that has no lifeguard dangerous?

14. Should you always go swimming with a friend?

練 習 三

B. 1. The father had three sons.

2. Yes, they were always quarreling.

3. Their father wanted them to be kind to one another.

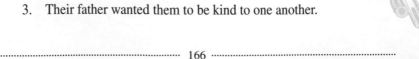

4. Their father showed them three sticks.

5. The father asked his sons to take the sticks, tie them together, and try to break the bundle of sticks.

6. The oldest son try with all his strength.

7. No, the oldest son could not break the bundle of sticks.

8. The other two could not break it either.

9. The father asked his sons to untie the bundle and take one stick and try to break it.

10. Yes, each son could break the stick easily.

11. The brothers could become as strong as the bundle when they worked together and helped one another.

12. They would be broken as easily as each of the sticks if they only quarreled and did not help one another.

練 習 四

A. 1. Yet her death had a profound effect on him.

2. To him, death was the worst of all evils.

3. But on the other hand, sticks and stones don't live either.

4. And live he did!

5. His life became somewhat of a legend.

6. He was born in Europe in 1865.

7. His early years in Europe intilled in him a deep joy for life.

8. This joy, however, was often tested during his first years in the United States.

9. Berenson's family immigrated to the United States in 1875.

10. His father became a wandering peddler in Boston.

11. The studying paid off.

12. Through writing books, selling, buying and telling others about the great masterpieces of Italian art, Berenson brought joy and beauty to other people.

練 習 五

A. 1. In the notes he asked his friends to help him, but it was useless.

2. He talked to people about the great need for a new government in China and he collected money to fight the old government.

3. in the year 1911 the old government of China was overthrown and a democratic one was established.

4. Dr. Sun became the first president of China, but there was still much quarreling.

B. 1. It was hot yesterday, so we went swimming.

2. I like swimming very much, and I can swim very well.

3. To learn swimming is not difficult, but it needs constant practice.

4. My sister wants to buy that toy very much, but she does not have enough money to buy it.

5. I went to bed late last night, so I did not get up until 10 o'clock this morning.

6. He felt no fear, for he was a brave man.

練 習 六

A. 1. Nowadays most people go to markets or modern supermarkets when they want to buy food. (副詞子句)

2. Modern man has forgotten how to survive in the wilderness where there are no markets. (名詞子句，副詞子句)

3. The wilderness is full of plants and animals which can be eaten. (形容詞子句)

4. But before someone eats these wild foods, he must first learn to follow one very important rule of the wilderness. (副詞子句)

5. This rule is that you must never eat a plant until you are certain that it is not harmful. (名詞子句，副詞子句)

6. There are very few places which do not yield some edible plant at least once a year. (形容詞子句)

7. Many of the cacti which grow in the desert can be eaten if they are properly prepared. (形容詞子句，副詞子句)

8. Plants are only one side of what the wilderness has to offer. （名詞子句）

9. If we follow the rules, we can once more discover the richness of nature's table. （副詞子句）

B. 1. There are many people who still buy food at the grocery.

2. Why don't you go to that supermarket where they're having a sale?

3. This lake is full of fish that can be eaten.

4. This is the gift he specially bought for you.

5. He is very grateful to you for what you have done for him.

6. He will call you as soon as he gets home.

練 習 七

A. 1. The exact reasons for this remain unclear, but it is known that age, sex, and occupation affect one's sensitivity to pain.

2. In general, women are more sensitive to pain than men; office workers are more sensitive than manual workers.

3. The persistent muscle tension that accompanies anxiety is thought to be a wide-spread source of pain and a vicious circle can develop: anxiety produces tension, tension produces pain, pain results in alarm and more anxiety, more anxiety results in

more pain, and so on.

B. 1. On her birthday, her father gave her a watch and her mother gave her a doll that looked like a real human being.

2. He has two older brothers: his first elder brother is a doctor, who is presently working in a hospital in Taipei, and his second elder brother is a lawyer, who is now practicing law in kaohsiung.

練 習 八

A. 1. Her father is a banker. (6)

2. The bus has arrived. (1)

3. There will be an exam tomorrow. (8)

4. It was raining hard. (2)

5. Miss Chang teaches English. (3)

6. The baby was crying. (1)

7. The teacher asked Tom a question. (4)

8. It was past midnight. (9)

9. The committee appointed Jack treasurer. (5)

10. She works in a bank. (2)

11. It is her birthday. (9)

12. That man is a dentist. (6)

13. The children remained at home. (7)

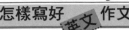

14. John is studying in the library. (2)

15. The manager bought the secretary a computer. (4)

16. There was a bundle of money in the box. (8)

17. The story is very interesting. (7)

18. The judge found him innocent. (5)

19. The author wrote a new book. (3)

20. That painting looks beautiful. (7)

B. 1. Her father is not a banker.

2. The bus has not arrived.

3. There will not be an exam tomorrow.

4. It was not raining hard.

5. Miss Chang does not teach English.

6. The baby was not crying.

7. The teacher did not ask Tom a question.

8. It was not past midnight.

9. The committee did not appoint Jack treasurer.

10. She does not work in a bank.

11. It is not her birthday.

12. That man is not a dentist.

13. The children did not remain at home.

14. John is not studying in the library.

15. The manager did not buy the secretary a computer.

16. There was not a bundle of money in the box.

17. The story is not very interesting.

18. The judge did not find him innocent.

19. The author did not write a new book.

20. That painting does not look beautiful.

C. 1. Is her father a banker?

2. Has the bus arrived?

3. Will there be an exam tomorrow?

4. Was it raining hard?

5. Does Miss Chang teach English?

6. Was the baby crying?

7. Did the teacher ask Tom a question?

8. Was it past midnight?

9. Did the committee appoint Jack treasurer?

10. Does she work in a bank?

11. Is it her birthday?

12. Is that man a dentist?

13. Did the children remain at home?

14. Is John studying in the library?

15. Did the manager buy the secretary a computer?

16. Was there a bundle of money in the box?

17. Is the story very interesting?

18. Did the judge find him innocent?

19. Did the author write a new book?

20. Does that painting look beautiful?

練 習 九

1. Prosperity makes friends, and adversity tries friends.

2. Mr.White has lost his wallet, and the whole family is upset.

3. Grace has a new doll, but she still prefers her old one.

4. The performance was poor, but the audience was enthusiastic.

5. Either they started late or they were delayed by some accident.

6. Hurry up or you will miss the train.

7. The Browns must be quite wealthy, for they go abroad every year.

8. Either you leave my house or I'll call the police.

9. I decided to stop and have lunch, for I was feeling quite hungry.

10. I had a headache, so I went to bed.

11. The shops were closed, so he couldn't get any bread.

12. She's clever girl, yet you can't help liking her.

練 習 十

A. 1. Scientists are interested in how people lived thousands of years

ago.

2. They want to find out what early peoples ate.

3. The carbon in the bones shows scientists what early peoples ate.

4. The carbon type found in their bones shows whether the people ate manioc or corn.

5. By knowing this, scientists can tell whether the people collected their food or grew it .

6. The carbon method also helps scientists find out what is in food today.

7. For example, one company said its honey was pure.

B. 1. I don't know where he bought that pen.

2. Ask your brother where he found it .

3. I'll find out how much he paid for it.

4. She wants to know when they are coming.

5. She will explain why Bob is absent.

6. I have no idea when they will arrive.

7. Nobody knows where they have gone.

8. Everyone knows that criticism often hurts others.

9. That you showed your superiosity will be resented.

10. The fact that you are right does not matter.

11. It is a fact that poetry is difficult for some readers.

12. That poetry must be read slowly is true.

練 習 十 一

1. He said that he wanted to help the people of his country.
2. He explained that a formal announcement would be made the following week.
3. He said that the poor man had been there almost a year.
4. Helen explained that that was why she had bought that old record.
5. Mary said that they liked to wear old-fashioned clothes.
6. He explained that this was a very special show.
7. She said that her husband wanted to move there.
8. He complained that it took him half a year to earn that much money.
9. Ralph said that it was the biggest race of the racing season.
10. Betty exclaimed that the waves looked pretty rough that day.
11. John asked where his bicycle was.
12. Jim asked whether I had seen his brother.
13. Tom asked what John bought the previous day.
14. He asked if I had finished my work.
15. She asked me whether I was going to the movies.
16. Peter asked me if the bus was coming.
17. He asked where I lost my key.

18. David asked how much the watch would cost.

19. She asked when he last wrote to me.

20. He asked why she was crying.

練 習 十 二

A. 1. However, the basic form of animation is the outlined figure that moves against an outlined background.

2. After a story has been decided upon, an artist-writer prepares a storyboard, which serves as the film's script.

3. It consists of rough sketches that show the action of the story, with the dialogue printed with each sketch.

4. After these decisions have been made, the layout artists prepare drawings to guide the other artists ,who will actually draw each scene.

B. 1. He has lost the key that fits all the doors.

2. That is the man from whom I bought the watch.

3. That pitcher who played last night was not very good.

4. I know the girl whose father owns the restaurant.

5. Do you know the name of the woman who saw the accident?

6. The bridge which crosses the river near the village is definitely unsafe.

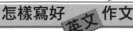
7. They caught a thief who has confessed.

8. I want to see the man who is in charge of production.

9. I have just been speaking to a man whose dog bit Bob yesterday.

10. The fire that started at six o'clock lasted for three hours.

C. 1. That is the taxi in which we came.

2. There is a shop in which I bought my watch.

3. David was the boy from whom I borrowed a book.

4. Those are the men to whom I sold the oranges.

5. Do you know the girl to whom Helen spoke?

6. That is the window from which he jumped.

7. This is the door through which the two men escaped.

8. The police have found the knife with which he was killed.

9. That is the boy with whom she was playing.

10. This is the bicycle which I rode last week.

D. 1. Do you see the lady with whom I ate lunch yesterday?

2. I have a friend who can help you.

3. The dog that wagged this tail was friendly.

4. The house where he lives is comfortable.

5. Those oranges, of which we ate four, were very sweet.

6. I walked outside where the sun was shining.

7. Was the vacation that you took last week pleasant?

8. She didn't remember the man's name which was difficult to pronounce.

9. I know a woman who lives on a boat.

10. Have you seen the club that has a large swimming pool?

練 習 十 三

A. 1. The area in a dog's brain concerned with smell is comparatively much larger than that in a man's brain. (表示程度)

2. When a dog smells an interesting or an unusual scent, is usually rapidly sniffs the air. (表示時間)

3. Thus many pet dogs can hear the family car approaching long before the human ear detects any sound at all. (表示時間)

4. If an object has no smell and is not moving, a dog may not even notice it . (表示條件)

5. Most hunting dogs do not see their prey until it moves. (表示時間)

B. 1. John has already entered a university, although he is only sixteen.

2. He studied hard in high school because he wanted to be accepted by a good university.

3. He always conducted himself properly as if he was older than his

4. Since his family lived a long way from a university, he had to move to a strange city.

5. When he reached the university, classes had not yet started.

6. While he was searching for a place to live, he met a foreign student.

7. After the two boys became acquainted, they decided to share a room.

8. The two boys decided to find an inexpensive place to live so that they could live with little money.

9. Unless they planned their expenditures carefully, they would not have enough money.

10. The two friends consulted the Dean before they looked for a room.

C. 1. Although the hill was steep, I rode up it.

2. Although it was very hot, we played basketball.

3. Although is was raining hard, they played football.

4. Although the watch was very expensive, he bought it.

5. Although she was late, she did not hurry up.

6. This watch is not accurate although I paid five thousand dollars for it.

7. Although I invited them, they did not come.

8. We managed to get to school although the road was flooded.

D. 1. When she had dug a hole, she buried the trash.

2. When we had finished playing football, we had an iced drink.

3. When the plane had landed safely, most of the passengers got off.

4. After she had washed the fruit, she gave us some.

5. Jim and I dried the car after John had washed it.

6. It began to rain a few minutes after she had hung out the clothes.

7. We arrived in Singapore three days after we had left Taiwan.

8. He had a rest after he had finished repairing the wall.

9. When she had finished the letter, she mailed it.

10. When I had turned off the tap, I started to repair the washing machine.

練 習 十 四

1. The river overflowed its banks and flooded the farmer's fields which he had just planted.

2. Since she was doing poorly in math. Sue hired a tutor who was a college student majoring in math.

3. Jogging, which is a form of exercise and popular all over the world, is very good for one's health.

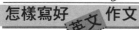

English

基 礎 入 門 篇

怎樣寫好 英文 作文

4. Energy conservation, which can save money, is very important, for the world's natural resources are limited.

5. Thinking about her boyfriend, from whom she hadn't heard for several days, she decided to write him a letter.

6. My elder brother, who is a college student, does his homework at night, and he concentrates on what he does so intently that he doesn't notice me when I enter his room.

7. Awakened by a strange noise, Mike leaped out of bed, went to investigate, and discovered a burglar who was trying to climb over the wall.

8. John and Mary attended the concert held at the Dr. Sun Yat-sen Memorial Hall and enjoyed all of the songs; their favorite song "Killing Me Softly" was sung at the end of the show.

9. Feeling a little hungry one evening, Allen went out to the local noodle stand where he ran into an old friend whom he hadn't seen for several months, and he didn't return home until midnight.

10. Jack, a businessman, is my neighbor; he works hard all week but relaxes on Sunday, and his favorite pastime is fishing.

11. The store built by my brother is a small one in which I cannot sell many things and there is not enough room for the customers.

12. There was a pretty girl, whose name was May, living in a village called Ta Nan; she was very kind to her neighbors, who liked her

very much because of her kindness.

13. The hall was so crowded that there were many men and women standing and sitting.

14. When the sun set, the sky grew cloudy, the lightning flashed, the thunder rumbled, and it rained, he hurried home.

15. Last night I had a nightmare, a dreadful one, which I can still remember though it did not last long.

16. Being in a hurry, he was driving so fast that he nearly knocked down an old woman who was crossing the road.

17. As we reached the island and landed, we could not see anybody except many birds that made a lot of noise, but they flew away when we went near them.

18. She takes care of her family so well that she never loses her temper and works very hard.

19. At ten o'clock the weather was cold, the sky was blue, and the moon shone brightly.

20. We could see colorful fish swimming in the water that was crystal clear.

21. My aunt, who lives in Taichung, came to us last week.

22. Walking through fields and along trails for most of the afternoon, we were hungry, and did not talk to each other.

23. Being the youngest child in the family, Helen is a six-year-old lovely girl, and her mother loves her very much.

24. He took the culprits to the police station on Ho-ping East Road where there was a police officer who thanked him very much.

25. She asked him how much the camera was and he replied that it cost two thousand dollars.

練 習 十 五

1. Born in London about 1340, Chaucer was the first great English poet.

2. Their lunches being all packed, the children are ready to go.

3. Being negligent, the parents allowed the boy to act as he pleased.

4. She has won almost all the prizes.

5. He enjoys nearly every motion picture he sees.

6. I can hear only a low mumble of voices.

7. She saw a beautiful dress of black lace in the shop window.

8. Gloria, whose mother studied nursing as a girl, is now thinking of becoming one herself.

9. Bruce said that my brother wasn't eligible.

10. Stevens, the writer, died in the hospital after an automobile accident.

練 習 十 六

1. Having drunk our sodas, we reached the platform as the train left.

2. After listening to the speaker for a few minutes, I allowed my thoughts to wander.

3. We saw the forest covered with a mantle of snow.

4. Rising to face his audience, Jack forgot every word of his prepared speech.

5. By smiling cheerfully, you can often chase away a gloomy mood.

6. While fishing today, I had my hook tangled in a mass of seaweed.

7. Arriving at Taipei, he found that the city was so large that he was frightened.

8. Cooled by air conditioning, this room could be made quite comfortable.

9. Seeing Jenny at the station, he was overwhelmed with surprise.

10. After driving several miles, we found from the sign that we were going in the wrong direction.

練 習 十 七

A. 1. Laughing gaily, Mary turned away.

2. Shaking his fist at me, Tom walked back to the car.

3. Abandoned by everyone, the child was weeping bitterly.

4. Watching his chance, the thief suddenly leaped for the window.

B. 1. Reading a vivid description brings us pleasure.

2. Choosing words wisely can create vivid pictures, too.

3. Being critical of one's own work is important.

4. The training of dogs is a highly skilled profession.

C. 1. He made a bad mistake to reject his father's help.

2. It was impossible for him to return home earlier.

3. He came to tell her the news.

4. We heard them call for help.

練 習 十 八

A. 1. Quickly and surely the boxer struck his opponent.

2. Everywhere in the room was disorder.

3. Faith, hope, and charity are three Christian principles.

4. Beautifully sang the soloist.

5. Great is the influence of television.

6. To the Chinese the honor for the world's first newspaper goes; the credit is well deserved.

7. Everywhere all over the world people want the latest news.

8. By newspapers surely life has been made richer.

9. To Mother it seemed silly to talk about things over and done with.

10. At the first of every month came the same old problem.

B. 1. It's John that I want to speak to.

It was Tom that broke the window yesterday.

2. You can't buy things without money.

He couldn't go without sleep for two nights.

3. She was so ill that we had to send for a doctor.

Father was so angry that he couldn't speak.

4. The thief ran so fast that we couldn't catch him.

She sang so well that the audience applauded for five minutes.

5. I've never seen such a man!

I hope I never have such an experience again.

6. His behavior was such that everyone disliked him.

His courage was such that he saved the old man from burning to death.

7. She had such a fright that she fainted.

He made such a mistake that he forgot her birthday.

練 習 十 九

A. 1. An air of calmness filled the valley. Enclosing the valley with wide green arms, the mountains seemed to protect it securely from the outside world. Two or three farmhouses slept in the sun. A cow or two under the trees of the pasture ate contentedly. The tiny white church surrounded by its little graveyard accentuated the quiet of the scene. *Truly, it seemed a place in which one might find peace.*

2. *The accident rate that winter was frightening.* Three of our lumbermen were struck by falling trees, eight were cut by saws, and two had their hands cut off by tractor treads. As many as fifteen lumbermen were gashed by axes each month. The insurance report at the end of the season showed a total of 102 injuries, all of them, fortunately, nonfatal.

3. The older I grow, the more I appreciate children. Now, on my 80th birthday, I salute them again, *Children are the most wholesome part of the human race, the sweetest, for they are freshest from the hand of God.* Playful, creative, mischievous, they fill the world with joy and good humor. We adults live a life of worry as to what they will think of us; a life of defense against their terrifying energy; a life of hard work to live up to their great

expectations. We put them to bed with a sense of relief—and greet them in the morning with delight and anticipation. We envy them the freshness of adventure and the discovery of life. In all these ways, children add to the wonder of being alive. In all these ways, they help to keep us young.

練 習 二 十

A.

_d_ 1. She was very understanding, but it didn't happen again.

_f_ 2. I brought them here with me and shall keep them in my heart forever.

_a_ 3. The first section stayed in the same room, the second went to another.

_e_ 4. No, I will never forget those warm and wonderful memories.

_c_ 5. All of us, is a delightful mood, stood giggling and choking with laughter as our teacher searched for us up and down the stairways!

_b_ 6. I remember that, on one April Fool's Day, fifteen girls hid in a corner of the hall instead of reporting to our room.

B.

_c_ 1. I look in the mirror and see the beginnings of a beard.

 a 2. Man makes elaborate plans for the future because he realizes that all too soon it will be the present.

 e 3. Being drawn back into reality, I think of the future.

 d 4. When I look back on the past seventeen years of my life, it seems like one day with many events crowded into it.

 f 5. I plan for the day when it will be the present.

 d 6. Only a minute ago I was learning long division; I thought high school was a hallowed place never to be attained.

C.

 d 1. No one knew what could be expected from it; but it was my own idea and my own invention, and I had to test it.

 b 2. A warm beam of light had fallen upon my face.

 e 3. My mind was about to collapse under the intense strain.

 a 4. It was a bright sunny day when I awoke.

 c 5. This morning might be my last; this was the thought that constantly went through my mind, for today was the day that I was to test the new machine.

練 習 二 十 一

A. Some people remember the things they are supposed to do by writing notes to themselves. *Then* they leave the notes in obvious

places, such as on the kitchen counter or on the floor in the middle of the living room. I've never been convinced that writing notes to myself does much good. Most of the time I lose them or forget to look at them until it's too late. I prefer to use an alarm clock to remind myself of things I'm supposed to do. I have ten alarm clocks in my house which I use to remind myself about things. *For example*, if I have to make a telephone call at a certain time, I'll set an alarm clock to go off a few minutes early and put the clock by the telephone. Or if I want to watch a certain television program, I'll set an alarm clock at the right time and put the clock on top of the TV set. I can remember almost anything I want to if I use my clocks. There is, *however*, one drawback to my system. Sometimes an alarm goes off and I don't know what it means. I always remember setting it, *but* not why I set it. If the clock is by the telephone, I know I may have set it to remind me to call someone, *but* I can't be sure. I might have set it to remind myself that somebody was to call me at a certain time.

B.   Curiosity is a good, positive reason for deciding to travel. Friends take trips and tell interesting stories about the people and places. *Therefore*, curious people want to learn by traveling, learning through their own experience. They buy tickets and go off to new places where they find unusual situations and adventure. They *also* find out some things about themselves.

However, there are some people who travel with another reason in mind. These people are traveling away from real troubles toward imagined solutions. People with problems at home sometimes travel to get away from such problems. Emerson's words are important to these people. Emerson meant that on a trip a traveler might be looking for a better situation or for an improvement. *Yet*, Emerson believed, the person will find only the happiness that he or she brought along. There are no new supplies in new places.

There are many inferences that can be made from Emerson's words. *For example*, a good student at home will be a good student abroad. A person who likes other people and was well-liked at home will find friends all over the world. *Furthermore* a troubled person will not find true answers—only temporary distractions. Travel will provide other things to think about, *but* the real problems do not disappear. Travel can *indeed* help a person to broaden horizons; travel can satisfy curiosity and make a person more aware of problems and possible solutions.

練 習 二 十 二

1. He said ,"I propose to transfer at the end of the semester."

2. Dr. J. A. Frazer was born on March 18, 1901.

3. Dr. Koch, a German scientist, discovered the tuberculosis bacillus.

4. The lecturer was the Rev. Nelson Laird, D. D.

5. Have you read his latest book?

6. The manuscript was dirty blotched and unevenly typed.

7. I have not seen him since his wife left; he has been keeping to himself.

8. Mr. Reynolds, the insurance man, called.

9. She is quite inexperienced and has never worked in an office before.

10. See the new revolutionary car of the year, the Ford.

11. She said, "When I asked his opinion, he answered, 'I don't give advice on such questions.'"

12. I am enclosing eighty-five dollars ($85.00) for the semiannual premium.

13. He looked at it enviously. "It's a beauty," he exclaimed.

14. However, I still have five payments to make.

15. That she won't like it may be taken for granted.

16. "Do you think he will accept?" she asked.

17. Ladies and gentlemen, it is a privilege to speak to you.

18. Aftre they took off from the airport, we felt very sad.

19. Of course, she explained, he will be here only a few days.

20. The singular form is "mouse"; the plural form is "mice".

21. A day's work well-done is a stepping-stone to the success of the following day's work.

22. Jim presented a well-planned program at the club meeting yesterday.

23. There were twenty-two members in attendance.

24. The Johnson's take pride in their neatly-trimmed lawn.

25. There is much give -and -take in our classroom discussions.

怎樣寫好英文作文─應用進階篇

主編：吳奚真
合編：張先信、Phillip Podgur
定價：220元

英文教學要培養四種基本能力：聽的能力、閱讀的能力、口頭表達能力、和文字表達能力。英文作文屬於文字能力的表達，就文字能力的表達而言，最根本的辦法當然是從培養語言習慣做起，很自然的養成基本的表達能力，對於中學生而言，這種能力的培養有賴於有意的「記憶」和「模仿」。本書針對中學生在學習英文作文方面，提供了一套完整的學習模式，從句子的形式、基本句形，句子的組合……由淺入深，循序漸進。書中各章並附有練習，熟讀本書必能讓你在英文作文的學習方面達到良好的效果。

大地 Learning 叢書介紹

英語散文集錦

編譯：吳奚真
定價：170元

本書選擇精簡散文29篇。部份選自吳教授在師大講授英國散文之教材，或由其翻譯之書籍中摘出。原文與譯文均極優美，並對立身處世之道有啟發，為自修英文與增進修養之最佳讀物

怎樣**寫好**
英文作文

怎樣 **寫好**
英文作文

國家圖書館出版品預行編目資料

怎樣寫好英文作文. 基礎入門篇／張先信,
Phillip Podgur 編著. -- 一版. -- 臺北
市：大地, 2003〔民92〕
　　面；　公分-- （Learning；6）

ISBN 957-8290-76-4（平裝）
1. 英國語言－作文－教學法　2. 中等教育

524.383　　　　　　　　　　92002357

Learning 06

怎樣寫好英文作文‧基礎入門篇

編　　著：張先信，Phillip Podgur

主　　編：吳奚眞

創 辦 人：姚宜瑛

發 行 人：吳錫清

美術編輯：普林特斯資訊有限公司

出 版 者：大地出版社

社　　址：台北市內湖區瑞光路358巷38弄36號4樓之2

劃撥帳號：50031946（戶名：大地出版社有限公司）

電　　話：(02)2627－7749

傳　　真：(02)2627－0895

E - m a i l：vastplai@ms45.hinet.net

印 刷 者：普林特斯資訊股份有限公司

一版四刷：2010年7月

定　　價：180元